STEWART BROWN was born in Southampton in 1951. After training to be a teacher he worked in a secondary school in Jamaica. He returned to Britain to study Fine Art and Literature at Falmouth School of A~~~ ~~~~ ~~~~~~~~~ studies at Sussex University and t Aberystwyth. Between times he w Caribbean and West Africa, lectu University, Kano, in northern Nig Lecturer in African and Caribbea West African Studies, University of Birmingham. In 1991 he spent a semester at the University of the West Indies, Cave Hill, Barbados.

Stewart Brown has published two collections of his own poetry, *Zinder* (1986) and *Lugard's Bridge* (1989), both from Seren Books, and edited two poetry anthologies, *Caribbean Poetry Now* (Hodder & Stoughton, 1985) and, with Mervyn Morris and Gordon Rohlehr, *Voiceprint* (Longman, 1989). In 1990 he edited a collection of Caribbean short stories, *Caribbean New Wave* (Heinemann), and in 1991 published *The Art of Derek Walcott* (Seven Books), a collection of essays.

IAN McDONALD is Antiguan and St Kittian by ancestry, Trinidadian by birth, Guyanese by adoption, and describes himself as West Indian by conviction. After gaining an honours degree in history at Cambridge, he returned to the Caribbean in 1955, settling in the then British Guiana where he has lived and worked ever since. As a world class sportsman, he played in and captained the West Indies Lawn Tennis team in the Davis Cup for many years.

During a distinguished career in the sugar industry, Ian McDonald has also contributed greatly to the Caribbean literary scene, not least as editor of a leading West Indian magazine, *Kyk-over-al*. He is a fellow of the Royal Society of Literature, and in 1991 was appointed Editorial Consultant to the West Indian Commission.

Many of his own works have been published, including *The Hummingbird Tree* (Heinemann, 1969), which won him the Royal Society of Literature Prize; two widely acclaimed collections of poems, *Mercy Ward* (1988), and *Essequibo* (1992), both from Peterloo Poets.

In 1986, McDonald received the Guyana National Honour, the Golden Arrow of Achievement.

THE HEINEMANN BOOK OF CARIBBEAN POETRY

Selected by Stewart Brown
and Ian McDonald

HEINEMANN

Heinemann Educational Publishers
Halley Court, Jordan Hill, Oxford OX2 8EJ
A Division of Reed Educational & Professional Publishing Limited

Heinemann: A Division of Reed Publishing (USA) Inc.
361 Hanover Street, Portsmouth, NH 03801-3912, USA

OXFORD   MELBOURNE   AUCKLAND
JOHANNESBURG   BLANTYRE   GABORONE
IBADAN   PORTSMOUTH (NH) USA   CHICAGO

First published by Heinemann International Literature
and Textbooks in 1992

British Library Cataloguing in Publication Data
A catalogue record for this book is available from the British Library.

ISBN 0 435 98817 4

Phototypeset by Wilmaset, Birkenhead, Wirral
Printed and bound in Great Britain by
Cox & Wyman Ltd, Reading, Berkshire

00   01   02   10 9 8   7   6   5

CONTENTS

ACKNOWLEDGEMENTS

The editors and publishers would like to thank the following for their permission to use copyright material:

John Agard, c/o Caroline Sheldon Literary Agency, for 'Pan Recipe' from *Man to Pan* (Ediciones Casa de las Americas, 1982), 'By All Means Bless' from *Lovelines For a Goatborn Lady* (Serpent's Tail, 1990); John Agard, c/o Serpent's Tail, for 'English Girl Eats Her First Mango' from *Mangoes and Bullets* (Serpent's Tail, 1985); Edward Baugh for 'Old Talk, or West Indian History' which appeared in *Graham House Review*, Spring 1991, 'Getting There' and 'The Carpenter's Complaint' from *A Tale from the Rainforest* (Sandberry Press, 1988); Louise Bennett for 'Home Sickness', 'Jamaican Oman', 'Love Letter' from *Selected Poems*, 1982 (used by permission of Sangster's Book Stores Ltd); James Berry and New Beacon Books for 'Lucy's Letter' from *Lucy's Letter and Loving* (New Beacon Books, 1982). 'It's Me Man', 'Fantasy of an African Boy' from *Chain of Days*, 1985 (Reprinted by permission of Oxford University Press); James Berry for 'One' from *When I Dance* (Hamish Hamilton Children's Books, 1988); Edward Kamau Brathwaite for 'Miss Own' from *Mother Poem*, 1977, 'Red Rising' from *Sun Poem*, 1982 and 'Xango' from *X/Self*, 1987 (Reprinted by permission of Oxford University Press), 'Naima' from *Jah Music*, 1986 (Used by permission of Savacou Publications); Jean Binta Breeze and Race Today Publications for 'Natural high', 'Dreamer' and 'Lovin wasn easy' from *Riddym Ravings*, 1988; Bloodaxe Books Ltd for 'Beacon of Hope' from *Tings an Times: Selected Poems* by Linton Kwesi Johnson (Bloodaxe Books, 1991). Wayne Brown and Inprint Caribbean Ltd for 'Rilke', 'Words', and 'Song for a Tourist' from *Voyages* (1989); Jan Carew for 'The Dreamtime Lives Again' and 'Tiho, The Carib'; Martin Carter and Demerara Publications for 'Bitter Wood', 'A Mouth is Always Muzzled', 'After One Year', 'Childhood of a Voice', 'In a Small City at Dusk', 'Bent', 'Being Always' from *Selected Poems* (Demerara Publishers Ltd, 1990); Brian Chan and Peepal Tree Books for 'Paradise' and 'How to Organise a Successful Small Business' from *Thief with Leaf* (Peepal Tree Books, 1988); Faustin Charles for 'Letters from Home'; Sebastian Clarke for 'Soucouyant' from *Douens* (1981); Merle Collins and Karia Press for 'Because the Dawn Breaks' and 'Trapped' from *Because the Dawn Breaks* (1985); Christine Craig for 'City Blues'; Cyril Dabydeen and Peepal Tree Books for 'Patriot', 'The Husband' and 'Dubious Foreigner' from *Island Lovelier than a Vision* (1986); David Dabydeen and Dangaroo Press for 'Catching Crabs', 'Coolie Mother', 'Coolie Son', 'Miranda' from *Coolie Odyssey* (1990); Fred d'Aguiar and Chatto & Windus Ltd for 'Mama Dot's Treatise' from *Mama Dot* (1985) and 'Airy Hall's Exits' and 'The Cow Perseverance' from *Airy Hall* (1989); Mahadai Das and Demerara Publications for 'Learner' and 'The Leaf in his Ear' from *Kyk-over-All*. Mahadai Das and Peepal Tree Books for 'Horses' and 'The Growing Tip' from *Bones* (1988); Gloria Escoffery for 'After the Fall', and 'Tricks of the Trade' from *Loggerhead* (Sandberry Press, 1988) and 'Mother Jackson Murders the Moon' (*Jamaica Journal*, Spring 1992); John Figueroa for 'Epitaph' and 'This tree my time keeper'; Honor Ford-Smith for 'Lala: The Dressmaker' and 'Aux Leon . . . Women'; Anson Gonzalez for 'Gasparillo Remembered', first published in *Moksha: Poems of Light and Sound* (Diego Martin: New Voices, 1988), 'Little Rosebud Girl', first published in *Voices*, ed. Clifford Sealey, Port of Spain (1968) and 'First Friday Bell', first published in *Score* (Diego Martin: New Voices, 1972); Lorna Goodison and New Beacon Books for 'Keith Jarrett—Rainmaker' and 'Guinea Woman' from *I am Becoming My Mother* by Lorna Goodison (New Beacon Books Ltd, 1986) and 'Gleanings' from *Heartease* by Lorna Goodison (New Beacon Books, 1988); Jean L. Goulbourne for 'This is the Place Where . . .', first published in *New Voices* (Diego Martin, 1984) and 'One Acre', first published in *Creation Fire* (Toronto, Sister Vision, 1990); Cecil Gray for 'The Misses Norman' and 'Funeral Service'; A. L. Hendriks and Hippopotamus Press for 'Where it's at', 'Jamaican Small Gal' and 'Cirrhosis' from *To Speak Simply: Selected Poems 1961–1986*; Kendel Hippolyte for 'revo lyric', 'the air between us', 'a caribbean exorcism poem' and 'Reggae Cat'; Abdur-Rahman Hopkinson and Peepal Tree Books for 'origami' and 'The Chord'; Arnold Itwaru

for 'and in this carnival' and 'body rites'; Amryl Johnson for 'Granny in de Market Place',
'And Sea' from *Tread Carefully in Paradise* (Cofa Press, 1991) and 'Gifts'; Linton Kwesi
Johnson for 'Beacon of Hope'; E McG. Keane and Cesa de les Americas for 'Week Seven'
from *One a Week with Water* and E McG. Keane for 'Soufrière' from *Volcano Suite*
(1979); Paul Keens-Douglas for 'Trinidad if ah let yu' and 'Wukhand'; Anthony Kellman
and Peepal Tree Books for 'Bajan' and 'The King' from *Watercourse* (1990); Jane King for
'Clichés for an Unfaithful Husband', 'Hymn' and 'Moments'; John Robert Lee and Phelps
Publications for 'Lusca' and 'Vocation' from *Saint Lucian, Selected Poems 67–87* and
John Robert Lee for 'Mango'; E. A. Markham for 'Herstory' from *Towards the End of a
Century* (Anvil Press Poetry, 1989), and 'Don't Talk to Me about Bread' from *Human
Rites* (Anvil Press Poetry, 1984); Marc Mathews for 'Realaroo' and 'Come Come';
Marina Ama Omowale Maxwell for 'Our Revolutions Must Be Different' published in
The New Voices (1984) and 'I Expect an Orchid'; Ian McDonald and Peterloo Poets for
'Life/Death', 'The Place they have to go' from *Mercy Ward* (1988), and 'The Poison-
maker' from *Essequibo* (1992); Anthony McNeil and Savacou Publications for 'Straight
Seeking' and 'Hello Ungod' from *Reel from The Life Movie* (1972). Anthony McNeil and
Jamaica Publications Ltd for '[write through the night]' and '[Olive]' from *Credences at
the Altar of Cloud* (1979); Mark McWatt and Dangaroo Press for 'Stone', 'A Man in the
House', 'The Boat Builder' and 'Lady Northcote' from *Interiors* (1989); Pauline Melville
and Dangaroo Press for 'Stonebridge Park Estate' and 'Homeland' from *Rented Rooms*
(ed. D. Dabydeen, 1988) and Pauline Melville for 'Honor Maria'; Ras Michael for
'Preface'; Rooplall Monar and Peepal Tree Books for 'Judgement Day' and 'Koker' from
Koker (1987); Pamela Mordecai for 'Easy Life', and 'Last Lines' from *Journey Poem*
(Sandberry Press) and 'Starapple Tree'; Mervyn Morris for 'Joseph of Arimathaea' and
'Pilate'; Mervyn Morris and New Beacon Books for 'Pre-Carnival Party', 'Swimmer' and
'Give T'anks' from *Shadow Boxing* (1979), and 'The Day My Father Died' from *The
Pond* (1973); Philip Nanton for 'I'; Grace Nichols and Virago Press for 'Tropical Death'
from *The Fat Black Woman's Poems* (1984) and 'Wherever I Hang' and 'Tapestry' from
Lazy Thoughts of a Lazy Woman (1989), Grace Nichols and Karnak House for 'Sugar
Cane' from *The Fat Black Woman's Poems* (1984); Sasenarine Persaud and Peepal Tree
Books for 'Rain Storm' from *Demerary Telepathy* (1988); Velma Pollard for 'Belize Suite'
and 'Su Su' from *Crown Point* (Sandberry Press, 1988); Marian Questel for 'Judge
Dreadword' and 'The Bush' by Victor Questel, © Marian Questel, first published in *Hard
Stares* (New Voices, Diego Martin, 1982). 'Near Mourning Ground' © Marian Questel,
first published in *Near Mourning Ground* (New Voices, Diego Martin, 1979); Rajandaye
Ramkissoon-Chen for 'Father' and 'When the Hindu Woman Sings Calypso'; Andrew
Salkey for 'Away' and 'A Song for England'. Andrew Salkey and Black Scholar Press for
'Inside' from *In The Hills Where Her Dreams Live*; Dennis Scott and New Beacon Books
for 'Apocalypse dub' and 'Dreadwalk' from *Dreadwalk* (1982). Mrs Joy Scott, Executor
of the Estate of Dennis Scott for 'Marrysong' from *Strategies* (Sandberry Press, 1989) The
University of Pittsburgh Press for 'Epitaph' © Dennis Scott 1973, from *Uncle Time* by
Dennis Scott; Olive Senior for 'Birdshooting Season', 'Searching for Grandfather', 'To the
Madwoman in my Yard', 'Hill Country' and 'Children's Hospital' from *Talking of Trees*
(Calabash Publications, 1985); Elma Seymour (widow of A J Seymour) for 'Name Poem',
'To The Family Home Awaiting Repair' and 'Millionaire' from *Collected Poems* (in
press); Jonathan Small for 'Pig-sticking Season' and 'Eating the Elephant Whole'; Michael
Smith and Race Today Publications for 'A Go Blow Fire', 'Black and White', 'Dis-ya
Dutty' and 'Revolutionary'; Ralph Thompson and Peepal Tree Books for 'He knows what
Height is'; Derek Walcott and Faber & Faber Ltd for 'Midsummer LIV', 'The Season of
Phantasmal Peace', 'Elsewhere' and 'The Hotel Normandie Pool' from *Collected Poems*
(Faber & Faber Ltd, 1989).

INTRODUCTION

The publisher's brief for this anthology was that it should represent 'simply the best' in West Indian poetry. To which the anthologists' only possible response had to be 'No Problem'! As editors, though, we were faced with the complexity of trying to define what 'the best' might mean in an arena of word culture where the very language of poetry is the subject of profound social, historical and political debate, where the cultural inputs are so diverse, where notions of form, craft and style are so contentious and where the cassette and the DJ are becoming as central to the dissemination and discussion of poetry as the literary magazine and the critic.

Without wishing to open old wounds it is instructive to look at the work of the two dominant figures in contemporary West Indian poetry, Derek Walcott and Edward Kamau Brathwaite, even as they are represented in this anthology, just to get some sense of the diversity of forms, of attitudes to language, of notions of purpose and of the sheer range of cultural referents to which contemporary West Indian poetry lays claim. Walcott set out to 'prolong the mighty line of Marlowe and Milton' and to add a distinctively West Indian voice to that Great Tradition. No one could dispute that he has achieved that ambition, with all it means in terms of the cultural matrix inscribed at the heart of his work. He has described the English language in the Caribbean as one of 'the spoils of history' and, while his work can sing off the page, his is very much a 'literary' poetry. Brathwaite, on the other hand, took as his models the griots of West Africa, the jazz and blues men of the American South, the calypsonians and the 'folk songs' of the plantation experience. His work is as dense with allusions to those traditions as Walcott's is with allusions to European

literature and classical mythology. Brathwaite set out to
'break English', to defend and extend the notion of
'nation language' as the medium of a Caribbean poetry.
His work repays careful scrutiny on the page but lives in
its enunciation, its oral dimension. Add to that diversity
of approaches the experience, voices and forms of a poet
like David Dabydeen who draws very much on the East
Indian heritage in the Caribbean, and the ways that the
many women poets who have come to prominence across
the region in the last decade bring notions of crafting and
ways of saying – as well as concerns and perspectives –
that are gender specific. . . . Then you have some notion
of the formal and cultural variety of West Indian poetry
now.

It is that range and variety that we have set out to
represent in this anthology. West Indian poetry has been
well served with anthologies in the last few years;
historical surveys like Paula Burnett's *Penguin Book of
Caribbean Verse*, thematic school anthologies like
Ramchand and Gray's *West Indian Poetry* and Brown's
Caribbean Poetry Now, higher level teaching texts like
Markham's *Hinterland*, collections representing
particular islands like Pamela Mordecai's *From Our
Yard: Jamaican Poetry Since Independence* or Margaret
Watt's anthology of poems by women from Trinidad and
Tobago, *Washer Woman Hangs Her Poems in the Sun*.
There have been several anthologies of poems exclusively
by women, most notably the pan-Caribbean selection in
Ramabai Espinet's *Creation Fire*. Other anthologies have
represented a particular strand in West Indian poetry like
Brown, Morris and Rohlehr's *Voiceprint; oral and related
poetry from the Caribbean*, while the exile experience is
chronicled in James Berry's *News for Babylon* and, in
Canada, Cyril Dabydeen's *A Shapely Fire*.

So what is distinctive about *this* anthology? What we
have tried to do in this selection is offer both the new

reader of West Indian poetry and confirmed readers who
share our conviction that West Indian poetry is one of
the real growing points of contemporary writing, a cross-
section of current practice, as it were. We have avoided
the standard anthology pieces – all the established poets
are represented here by recent work – and we have
included poems by many writers whose work has not
appeared in major anthologies before. We have not set
out to demonstrate a thesis nor to group poets or poems
by theme, style or even period or region. But neither is
this, on the other hand, a simple 'democratic' anthology
in terms of trying to represent all the islands and
territories in the Caribbean fairly, nor in terms of trying
to balance the ethnic, gender or cultural inputs that are
represented. There are, literally, hundreds of West Indian
poets writing now whose work we were not able –
because of inevitable limitations of space – to include in
this selection, and the omission of such figures as
Howard Fergus of Montserrat, Willi Chen of Trinidad,
John Gilmore of Barbados, David Williams of Jamaica
and Stanley Greaves of Guyana, to name just a few, has
caused us much heartache. We did, though, want to
emphasise the achievements of particular poets whose
work is sometimes overshadowed by the 'big two'
presentation of West Indian poetry, hence the space given
to the work of Mervyn Morris, Martin Carter and,
among younger poets, Kendel Hippolyte, Olive Senior
and Mahadai Das. In the end we did have to trust to our
own judgement of what was 'simply the best', being
conscious all the while that the anthologists' power –
particularly in this kind of broad representative
anthology – is finally the power to exclude. Samuel
Johnson remarked that 'every other author may aspire to
praise; the lexicographer can only hope to escape
reproach. . .' perhaps mere anthologists cannot even
hope for that!

We set ourselves several rules of selection, though most were broken from time to time. We limited ourselves to poems in English, or an English inflected creole, which immediately cut out more than half the Caribbean. A pan-Caribbean anthology would have been the ideal, but problems of translation aside, to begin to be 'representative' such an anthology would have to run to several volumes! The poets from whose work we selected were all alive and actively writing into the 1980s and have published at least one full collection of poetry. We determined to opt for recent work rather than the anthology standbys – see what a revelation the work of Martin Carter is here for those who know his work only by the anthology classics. We resisted taking extracts from long poems. We gave priority to poets based in and/ or who seemed to be writing *into* the Caribbean, and we selected poems that were primarily intended to be read off the page rather than heard or experienced in performance.

The last two limitations were the most problematic and may explain the omission of several writers who might otherwise be expected to be found here. There are, of course, many poets of Caribbean background now living in Canada, the UK and the USA – and indeed further afield. Some of them have chosen, reasonably enough in their circumstances, to focus their writing into those societies rather than out and back to the Caribbean. When push came to shove in the fight for space in this anthology some of them got squeezed out. Similarly, there is a movement of poets operating right across the Caribbean now for whom the text of a poem is only an *aide memoire*, a script for their performance, a kind of shadow-score that, without the experience of performance or at least the recording of what Professor Gordon Rohlehr has termed their personal voice print, has little inherent value. Of course many Caribbean poets

work the tension between voice and print most creatively
– from Louise Bennett through Edward Kamau
Brathwaite to John Agard, Lorna Goodison and Jean
Binta Breeze, but for all of them the poem as text is at
least as significant as the poem as voice, and yields to the
examination of readers. The works of poets like
Mutaburuka in Jamaica, Mike Richards in Barbados,
Malik in Trinidad or George 'Fish' Alphonse in Saint
Lucia, on the other hand, while admirable and indeed
often spellbinding in performance, often seem so thin *as
text* that to include them in this anthology would be to
do their work a dis-service. The anthology does include
work by several poets who are certainly best known for
essentially 'voice-poems' but they are represented here by
less familiar work that demonstrates the range of their
talents – look particularly at the selection from Michael
Smith in this regard.

After all the worrying and wrangling over the
selection, we do believe that this anthology offers its
readers a real sense of the energy, variety and
accomplishment of contemporary West Indian poetry.
One genuine cause, at least, in this 'Quincentennial'
period, for celebration. Many of the poets in the
anthology are represented by only one or two poems,
obviously not enough to give a real sense of their work
but enough, we hope, to whet readers' appetites. We
have tried, in the extensive Biographical Notes, to
provide enough biographical and bibliographical
information to set their work in some kind of personal
context and enable interested readers to pursue their
work further.

STEWART BROWN AND IAN MCDONALD
MAY, 1992

John Agard

English Girl Eats Her First Mango

a kind of love poem

If I did tell she
hold this gold
of sundizzy
tonguelicking juicy
mouthwater flow
ripe with love
from the tropics

she woulda tell me
trust you to be
melodramatic

so I just say
taste this mango

and I watch she hold
the smooth cheeks
of the mango
blushing yellow
and a glow
rush to she own cheeks

and she ask me
what do I do now
just bite into it?

and I was tempted
to tell she
why not be a devil
and eat of the skin
of original sin

but she woulda tell me
trust you to be
mysterious

so I just say
it's up to you
if you want to peel it

and I watch she feel it
as something precious

then she smile and say
looks delicious

and I tell she
don't waste sweet words
when sweetness
in you hand

just bite it man
peel it with the teeth
that God give you

or better yet
do like me mother
used to do
and squeeze
till the flesh
turn syrup
nibble a hole
then suck the gold
like bubby
in child mouth
squeeze and tease out
every drop of spice

sounds nice
me friend tell me

and I remind she
that this ain't
apple core
so don't forget
the seed
suck that too
the sweetest part
the juice does run
down to you heart

man if you see
the English rose
she face was bliss
down to the pink
of she toes

and when she finish
she smile
and turn to me

lend me your hanky
my fingers
are all sticky
with mango juice

and I had to tell she
what hanky
you talking bout
you don't know
when you eat mango
you hanky
is you tongue

man just lick
you finger
you call that
culture
lick you finger
you call that
culture

unless you prefer
to call it
colonization
in reverse

By All Means Bless

By all means
bless the cloth
that wiped
the face
of Jesus

By all means
bless the towel
that unfolds
an infant
like miraculous bread

By all means
bless the towel
the boxer returns to
– a brief harbour
after a harassing round

By all means
bless the sacred silk
that garbs
the sumo's
amplitude of loin

But I say this also
bless the towel
that unwraps
your buttocks
(fresh out of the shower)
with such casual ease

we overlook
life's small epiphanies

Pan Recipe

First rape a people
simmer for centuries

bring memories to boil
foil voice of drum

add pinch of pain
to rain of rage

stifle drum again
then mix strains of blood

over slow fire
watch fever grow

till energy burst
with rhythm thirst

cut bamboo and cure
whip well like hell

stir sound from dustbin
pound handful biscuit tin

cover down in shanty town
and leave mixture alone

when ready will explode

Edward Baugh

Old Talk, Or West Indian History

From Keith Laurence's gracious patio
on Santa Margarita Circular Road
we looked down on St. Augustine, the library
in darkness. Beyond, the line of car lights
traced the Butler Highway and beyond
the Plains of Caroni imagining the Ganges.
A BeeWee sunbird, wing weary, homes
to Piarco from island hopping all day
in the sun, from Norman Manley, Munoz
Marin, Vere Bird, Grantley Adams, which were once
more felicitously Palisadoes, Isla Verde
Coolidge Field, Seawell. Diminished at this distance
but doggedly a cane fire burns. It has been burning
for three hundred years. In the morning
as usual we shall brush the soot from the tablecloth
and the pillow. A light which illumines
nothing, our laughter breaks on this hillside,
cascades to meet the sound of silvered
steel ascending from a pan yard. Cut
their names in the bark of this verse: Woodville
Marshall, Keith Hunte, Bill and Nora
Mailer, Joy Pilgrim, Laurence, and the bearded
chief reveller at this wake, the onliest raconteur,
Augier, Roy, who would pronounce
the benediction on every late night lime.
'No, no, we ent going home: we ent
leaving, we ent going home to night.'
You never heard the same tale twice.
Augier's Veranda Talk, an archive
of loose leaves scattered up and down
the archipelago, which only the night wind

will research. In the library below us, the books
on their roosts of shelves twitter among themselves
like schoolboys in dormitories after lights out
about the futility of scribes and the passion
for fixing the past. Laurence, in his italic
style, tells a story how at election time
they dug the road up down the hill
to fix it, then dug it up again
to show how they could fix it: History as The Big Fix.
Roy, ex-Royal Air Force gunner
tells of sorties among sugar-apple vendors
in Kingston's Coronation Market – O
those imperial trades! Now hear this one:
Paradise is to kotch up with a book, eating
sugar apple under a sugar apple tree
and then old Omar Khayyam wouldn't
have nothing over we.
                              This settles nothing
fixes nothing; it is only what I remember
and what I made up, what I made. I wanted
something to remember them by, so I invented it.
At dawn the sunbird will lift from Piarco,
a busha bird riding out to count his plantations.
From the height of noon, over Hispaniola
you will look down through a clarity so absolute
it hurts – the brown land after
the denudations of history, the shining caravels
of clouds, each moored precisely over
its shadow, and even earth's hurt-
ling seems to have stopped. But you can't hold
this high; the engines' throb will cut through
any epiphany, always, ladies
and gentlemen, we are about to begin our descent.
Grip the arm rest and pray; smooth landings
mild evenings and gracious patios.

But man,
how you could ramble so! Yes, I had meant it
to be purposeful, like history, but is only old talk.

Getting There

It not easy to reach where she live.
I mean, is best you have a four-wheel drive,
and like how my patty pan so old
and spare parts hard to get, I fraid.
I wonder why that woman love
hillside so much and winy-winy
road, when everybody know
she born under Cross Roads clock and grow
by seaside like all the rest of we.
Some part, I tell you, two vehicle can't pass
and if rain falling is watercourse
you navigating, and rockstone mashing up
you muffler, and ten to one
a landslide blocking you. You must
keep you eye sharp for the turn-off
or you pass it and lost. I bet
by now you dying to know
who this woman I talking bout
so much! Well, to tell
the truth, I not too sure
myself. My friend who study
Literature say she is the tenth
muse. Him say her name
is Silence. I don't know
nothing bout that, but I want
to believe what them other one say
is true – that when you reach
you don't worry so much

bout the gas and the wear-and-tear
no more, and it have some flowers
and bird make your spirit repose
in gladness, and is like
everything make sense, at last.

The Carpenter's Complaint

Now you think that is right, sah? Talk the truth.
That man was mi friend. *I* build it, *I*
Build the house that him live in; but now
That him dead, that mawga-foot bwoy, him son,
Come say, him want a nice job for the coffin,
So him give it to *Mister* Belnavis to make –
That big-belly crook who don't know him arse
From a chisel, but because him is big-shot, because
Him make big-shot coffin, fi-him coffin must better
Than mine! Bwoy, it hot me, it hot me
For true. Fix we a nex' one, Miss Fergie –
That man coulda knock back him waters, you know sah!
I remember the day in this said-same bar
When him drink Old Brown and Coxs'n into
The ground, then stand up straight as a plumb-line
And keel him felt hat on him head and walk
Home cool, cool, cool. Dem was water-bird, brother!
Funeral? *Me*, sah? That bwoy have to learn
That a man have him pride. But bless mi days!
Good enough to make the house that him live in,
But not good enough to make him coffin!
I woulda do it for nutt'n, for nutt'n! The man
Was mi friend. Damn mawga-foot bwoy.
Is university turn him fool. I tell you,
It burn me, it burn me for true!

Louise Bennett

Home Sickness

Me dah dead fi drink some coaknut water,
See a breadfruit tree,
Lawd, fi walk eena de broilin sun
An bade eena de sea.

Me nyam cabbage an pittata chips
An gwan like seh me please,
But me belly dissa holler
Fi a plate a rice an peas,

Fi a dumplin, a duckoonoo,
Fi a bulla full a spice,
An fi cool me suganwater
Wid a quattie lump a ice.

An fi board a market train an hear
De people-dem a chat
Bout de good foot weh dem buck up
Or de bad dream weh dem got.

English country road-dem pretty
An sometime when me dah roam
An me see a lickle village
Me feel jus like me deh home.

But me galang an me galang,
Me no see no donkey cart!
Me no meet up no black smaddy,
An it heaby up me heart.

For me long fi see a bankra basket
An a hamper load
A number-leven, beefy, blacky,
Hairy mango pon de road!

An me mout-top start fi water,
Me mout-corner start fi foam;
A dose a hungry buckle-hole me
Am me waan fi go back home.

Go back to me Jamaica,
To me fambly! To me wha?
Lawd-amassi, me figat –
All a me fambly over yah!

Jamaica Oman

Jamaica oman cunny sah!
Is how dem jinnal so?
Look how long dem liberated
An de man dem never know!

Look how long Jamaica oman
– Modder, sister, wife, sweetheart –
Outa road an eena yard deh pon
A dominate her part!

From Maroon Nanny teck her body
Bounce bullet back pon man,
To when nowadays gal-pickney tun
Spellin-Bee champion.

From de grass root to de hill-top,
In profession, skill an trade,
Jamaica oman teck her time
Dah mount an meck de grade.

Some backa man a push, some side-a
Man a hole him han,
Some a lick sense eena man head,
Some a guide him pon him plan!

Neck an neck an foot an foot wid man
She buckle hole 'so-so rib'
While man a call her 'so-so-rib'
Oman a tun backbone!

An long before Oman Lib bruck out
Over foreign lan
Jamaica female wasa work
Her liberated plan!

Jamaica oman know she strong,
She know she tallawah,
But she no want her pickney-dem
Fi start call her 'Puppa'.

So de cunny Jamma oman
Gwan like pants-suit is a style,
An Jamaica man no know she wear
De trousiz all de while!

So Jamaica oman coaxin
Fambly budget from explode
A so Jamaica man a sing
'Oman a heaby load!'

But de cunny Jamma oman
Ban her belly, bite her tongue,
Ketch water, put pot pon fire
An jus dig her toe a grung.

For 'Oman luck deh a dungle',
Some rooted more dan some,
But as long as fowl a scratch dungle heap
Oman luck mus come!

Lickle by lickle man start praise her,
Day by day de praise a grow;
So him praise her, so it sweet her,
For she wonder if him know.

Love Letter

Me darlin love, me lickle dove,
Me dumplin, me gizada,
Me sweetie Sue, I goes fa you
Like how flies goes fa sugar.

As ah puts me pen to paper
An me pen-nib start fi fly
Me rememberance remember
De fus day yuh ketch me yeye!

Yuh did jus come off a tramcar,
A bus was to yuh right,
A car swips pass yuh lef aise,
An yuh tan up stiff wid fright.

Yuh jaw drop, yuh mout open,
Jus like when jackass start yawn;
Me heart go boogoo-boogoo,
An me know wha meck me bawn!

Do, no scorn me lickle letter;
No laugh after me, yaw —
Me learnin not too gran, so what
Me cyaan spell me wi draw!

De ting eena de corner wid
De freckles, is me heart;
An de plate wid yam an salfish mean
Dat we can never part.

See how me draw de two face-dem
Dah look pon one anodder?
Well, one is me an one is yuh —
Teck any one yuh rader.

Is not a cockroach foot dis,
Is a finger wid a ring!
An it mean me want fi married yuh,
Dis line is piece a string —

Teck it put roun de weddin finger
A yuh weddin han,
Careful fi get de right size,
An den gi it to dis man.

De man is me. Now, sweet rice,
Keep swell till ah see yuh nex.
Accept me young heart while ah close
Wid love an bans a x.

James Berry

It's Me Man

I wouldn't be raven
   though dressed so
I wouldn't bleed my last
   though crushed
I wouldn't stay down
   though battered
I wouldn't be convinced
   though worst man
I wouldn't stay pieces
   though dissected
I wouldn't wear the crown
   though king of rubbish
I wouldn't stay dead
   though killed
I wouldn't stay dead
   though killed

Fantasy of an African Boy

Such a peculiar lot
we are, we people
without money, in daylong
yearlong sunlight, knowing
money is somewhere, somewhere.

Everybody says it's a big
bigger brain bother now,
money. Such millions and millions
of us don't manage at all
without it, like war going on.

And we can't eat it. Yet
without it our heads alone
stay big, as lots and lots do,
coming from nowhere joyful,
going nowhere happy.

We can't drink it up. Yet
without it we shrivel when small
and stop forever
where we stopped,
as lots and lots do.

We can't read money for books.
Yet without it we don't
read, don't write numbers,
don't open gates in other countries,
as lots and lots never do.

We can't use money to bandage
sores, can't pound it
to powder for sick eyes
and sick bellies. Yet without
it, flesh melts from our bones.

Such walled-round gentlemen
overseas minding money! Such
bigtime gentlemen body guarded
because of too much respect
and too many wishes on them.

Too many wishes, everywhere,
wanting them to let go
magic of money, and let it fly
away, everywhere, day and night,
just like dropped leaves in wind!

Lucy's Letter

Things harness me here, I long
for we labrish* bad. Doors
not fixed open here.
No Leela either: No Cousin
Lil, Miss Lottie or Bro'-Uncle.
Dayclean doesn' have cockcrowin'.
Midmornin' doesn' bring
Cousin-Maa with her naseberry tray.
Afternoon doesn' give a ragged
Manwell, strung with fish
like bright leaves. Seven days
play same note in London, chile.
But Leela, money-rustle regular.

Me dear, I don' laugh now,
not'n' like we thunder claps
in darkness on verandah.
I turned a battery hen
in 'lectric light, day an' night.
No mood can touch one
mango season back at Yard.
At least though I did start
evening school once.
An' doctors free, chile.

London isn' like we
village dirt road, you know
Leela : it a parish
of a pasture-lan' what
grown crisscross streets,
an' they lie down to my door.
But I lock myself in.

*to gossip without restraint.

I carry keys everywhere.
Life here's no open summer,
girl. But Sat'day mornin' don'
find me han'dry, don' find me face
a heavy cloud over the man.

An' though he still have
a weekend mind for bat'n'ball
he wash a dirty dish now, me dear.
It sweet him I on the Pill.
We get money for holidays
but there's no sun-hot
to enjoy cool breeze.

Leela, I really a sponge
you know, for traffic noise,
for work noise, for halfway
intentions, for halfway smiles,
for clockwatchin' an' col' weather.
I hope you don' think I gone
too fat when we meet.
I booked up to come an' soak
the children in daylight.

One

Only one of me
and nobody can get a second one
from a photocopy machine.

Nobody has the fingerprints I have.
Nobody can cry my tears, or laugh my laugh
or have my expectancy when I wait.

But anybody can mimic my dance with my dog.
Anybody can howl how I sing out of tune.
And mirrors can show me multiplied
many times, say, dressed up in red
or dressed up in grey.

Nobody can get into my clothes for me
or feel my fall for me, or do my running.
Nobody hears my music for me, either.

I am just this one.
Nobody else makes the words
I shape with sound, when I talk.

But anybody can act how I stutter in a rage.
Anybody can copy echoes I make.
And mirrors can show me multiplied
many times, say, dressed up in green
or dressed up in blue.

Edward Kamau Brathwaite

Miss Own

I

Selling calico cloth on the mercantile shame-
rock, was one way of keeping her body and soul-seam together
surrounded by round-shouldered backras on broad street
by cold-shouldered jews on milk

market

in the dark ghetto store
the bolt of cloth tugged, turned, revolved upon its wooden
 thunder

revealing rivers of green beige and muslin
lightnings of foreigner factories, bourgs

sign a bill here

and the storewalker
plodding prodding

                indentured to the merchant's law
                the merchant's whip
                the merchant's weakly pay

comes

on his own flat foot to
sign the bill here
figures snakes and foxes

for some pampered child's penthouse apartment high above new
   york
listening, on her wheel of self-indulgent sorrow
to roberta flack

while our barrow boy calls
rags ole rags: cloze ole cloze
got any ole bottles today?

she sippin she drink
an i slippin out into de heat o de sun
to buy what me scrape from she barrel

2

selling half-soul shoes in the leather
department, was another good way of keeping her body and soul-
   seam together

toes: scorn: instep: honeycomb of boxes: stretch up: pull down:
   put down: open

the tanneries of morocco, of algeciras, sokoto, of boot
leg lacquered italy: buffalo and cow horn rumbling

into the stockyards of styx of chicago
abattoirs of spout and thunder: sloped slaughterhouses of the
   chamois studded bronx:

cries calls clanks butchers' halls' bulls' knives stretch-
ing up: pulling down: putting down: open-

ing up the blood of the in-
growing toe-nail: worship of creak and spine

ache

3

for the shoe is a safe cottage to the illiterate peasant
needing light, running water, the indestructible plastic of the soft
   ill
lit/erate present

sign a bill here

and she kneels before the altar of the golden calf
altering its tip and instep
keeping body an soul-seam together

and the merchant smiles, lost in his founderies
setting out on his barefooted pilgrimage
across the inverterate prairies

Xango

I

Hail

there is new breath here

huh

there is a victory of sparrows

erzulie with green wings

feathers sheen of sperm

hah

there is a west wind
sails open eyes the conch shell sings hallelujahs

i take you love at last my love
my night my dream my horse my gold/en horn my africa

softly of cheek now
sweet of pillow

cry
of thorn

pasture
to my fire

we word with salt this moisture vision
we make from vision

black and bone and riddim

hah

there is a gourd tree here
a boy with knotted snakes and coffle wires

a child
with water courses valleys clotted blood

these tendrils knitted to the cold
un

pearl and wail
the earth on which he steps breaks furl

in rain

bow

tears

the
tiger clue

is his

the bamboo
clumps the bougainvillea

bells

his syllables
taste of wood of cedar lignum vitae phlox

these gutterals
are his own mon general mon frere

his childhood of a stone
is rolled away he rings from rebells of the bone his liberated day

2

over the prairies now
comanche horsemen halt

it is the buff the brown the rose
that brings them closer

the thousand tangled wilful heads
bull yellow tossing

the stretch the itch the musk
the mollusc in the nostril

the flare of drum
feet plundering the night from mud to arizona

the bison plunge into the thunders river
hammering the red trail blazing west to chattanooga

destroying de soto francisco coronado

un
hooking the waggons john

ford and his fearless cow
boy crews j

p morgan is dead
coca cola is drowned

the statue of liberty's never been born
manhattan is an island where cows cruise on flowers

3

and all this while he smiles carved terra cotta
high life/ing in abomey
he has learned to live with rebellions

book and bribe
bomb
blast and the wrecked village

he is earning his place on the corner
phantom jet flight of angels
computer conjur man

he embraces them all

for there is green at the root of his bullet
michelangelo working away at the roof of his murderous rocket

he anointeth the sun with oil
star.tick.star.tick.crick.et.clock.tick

and his blues will inherit the world

4

he comes inward from the desert
with the sheriffs

he flows out of the rivers out of the water
toilets with shrimp and the moon's monthly oysters

he comes up over the hill/slide with grave
diggers he walks he walks

in the street with moonlight with whistles with police kleghorns
with the whores pisstle

5

after so many twists
after so many journeys
after so many changes

bop hard bop soul bop funk
new thing marley soul rock skank
bunk johnson is ridin again

after so many turns
after so many failures pain
the salt the dread the acid

greet

him
he speaks
so softly near

you

hear
him
he teaches

face
and faith
and how to use your seed and soul and lissom

touch
him
he will heal

you

word
and balm
and water

flow

embrace
him
he will shatter outwards to your light and calm and history

your thunder has come home

Red Rising

I

When the earth was made
when the wheels of the sky were being fashioned
when my songs were first heard in the voice of the coot of the owl
hillaby soufriere and kilimanjaro were standing towards me with
   water with fire

at the centre of the air

there
in the keel of the blue
the son of my song, father-giver, the sun/sum
walks the four corners of the magnet, caught in the wind, blind

in the eye of ihs own hurricane

and the trees on the mountain be-
come mine: living eye of my branches
of bone; flute
where is my hope hope where is my psalter

my children wear masks dancing towards me the mews of their
   origen earth

so that this place which is called mine
which will never know that cold scalpel of skull, hill of dearth

brain corals ignite and ignore it

and that this place which is called now
which will never again glow: coal balloon anthracite: into cross-

roads of hollows

black spot of my life: *jah*
blue spot of my life: *love*
yellow spot of my life: *iises*
red spot of my dream that still flowers flowers flowers

let us give thanks

when the earth was made
when the sky first spoke with the voice of the rain/bow
when the wind gave milk to its music
when the suns of my morning walked out of their shallow thrill/
   dren

2

So that for centuries now have i fought against these opposites
how i am sucked from water into air
how the air surrounds me blue all the way

     from ocean to the other shore
     from halleluja to the black hole of hell

     from this white furnace where i burn
     to those green sandy ant-hills where you grow your yam

you would think that i would hate eclipses
   my power powdered over as it were

     but it's hallucination my fine friend
     a fan a feather; some

     one else's breath of shadow
     the moon's cool or some plan/et's

     but can you ever guess how i
     who have wracked

you wrong
long too to be black

be
come part of that hool that shrinks us all to stars

how i
with all these loco

motives in me
would like to straighten

strangle eye/self out

grow a beard wear dark glasses
driving the pack straight far

ward into indigo and vi
olet and on into ice like a miss

ile

rather than this surrendered curve
this habit forming bicycle of rains and seasons
weathers when i tear my hair

i will never i now know make it over the atlantic of that nebula

but that you may live my fond retreating future
i will accept i will accept the bonds that blind me
turning my face down/wards to my approaching past these
   morning chill/dren

Naima

for John Coltrane

Propped against the crowded bar
he pours into the curved and silver horn
his old unhappy longing for a home

the dancers twist and turn
he leans and wishes he could burn
his memories to ashes like some old notorious emperor

of rome. but no stars blazed across the sky when he was born
no wise men found his hovel. this crowded bar
where dancers twist and turn

holds all the fame and recognition he will ever earn
on earth or heaven. he leans against the bar
and pours his old unhappy longing in the saxophone

Jean Binta Breeze

dreamer

  roun a rocky corner
by de sea
seat up
  pon a drif wood
yuh can fine she
gazin cross de water
a stick
  eena her han
tryin to trace
    a future
  in de san

natural high

my mother is a
red
woman

she
gets high
on clean children

grows
common sense

injects
tales
with heroines

fumes
over dirty habits

hits the sky
on bad lines

cracking meteors

my mother
gets red
with the sun

lovin wasn easy

lovin wasn easy all de time
sweet
but nat easy
some a de time

dung eena tavern
lite use to dim
pan rusty zinc
wen coir mattrass a scratch
but im finga
use to run ribba
pan de one foot piano
an wen im hit a rite note
two white rum wid im cousin
dung a shap

lovin wasn easy
wen de food run out
an de two pap chow jus cut
de evenings of bwoil rice
widdout salt
an de neighbour a cuss
bout we bedspring noise

neva even get easier
wen we bruk
eena de back room ova in Mona
wid roach a run racket wid de flour
troo de water cuts
de power cuts
de door weh couldn lack
we use to drif troo dreams
pan herb smoke
troddin freeplan mount'n

an even wen we reach dem
lovin wasn easy

de back breaking hoe to soil
sometimes wen a watch im
trow im fork
ah tink im was de debbil
washin worn out clothes
dung a ribba
heng dem out fi dry
pan bamboo
de way mi calf get big
a karry water up de hill

wasn easy at all

cep wen
warm
eena de tear up tent
a we blanket
jine wid we glue
we use to watch mawnin star
rise
troo de hole
eena de bamboo shack

an now
sometimes
ah sad
wen ah look back

Wayne Brown

Rilke

for Edna Manley

For seven years, eyesockets like caves,
he watched in the mountains over the city
for the coming of the printless beast. But
in his mind's known home, continued usual,
order undisturbed: the cushioned cat,
the twitching dog asleep on the mat,
and his fed fire, private, stern,
keeping its anguished monologue of coals,
small poems in the lessening light.

Now past his prime, he watched at night
the logbook thicken with his soul's
entries, the low controlled fire turn
strange shapes off its silent walls.
He could discern nothing. The flagged hall
echoed, vacant, gaunt. Outside, wind leapt
howling in the trees; an evil mist crept
inward. He rose and dragged his wooden chair
as close to the fire as he dared.
From here there was nowhere to go.
Would the animal never rise?

The poems, he knew now, were lies,
bright, hot-pawed, skittery cats
cuffing, triumphant, out of old corners
dead roaches into the light. Yet on nights
when the moon like water rose to his eyes
and the fire sank into its pit, some ghost-
dog's howl, old as the hills, would sink

inward on ribbons of wind, and, shaken, he
would think: 'Time for another log.' Might not

A little fire, small poem, save him?
Somewhere, someone was lying still
                                   So
for seven years he stayed, enfolded in mist
but mesmerised, dulled by that same fire's glare
that kept the animal out. But one night
exhausted, slept on his chest, coals
tiny as stars, and the animal entered.

All night in nightmare he dreamt of the wail
of the wind, taking new shapes within him
like flames; and next day was sure he'd glimpsed
(too briefly for charting, it left no trail)
the shadow of a great unkempt beast
bounding through billowing veils of mist,
the poem swung like a kite at its tail,

Crying in the teeth of the wind.

Words

(for his estranged wife)

Everything revolved at first, then settled
to an elate stillness.
You move, pristine through memory,
a stranger I have always known,
big-boned and careless and capable,
likelier than I was to stand than run,
pursued now by two dreamless daughters.

The only people in the world
you could never outface or outwait!
I know this is inappropriate,
that these lines, splaying, miss the ground
where you dream, a distracted, vague tree
or felon for her freedom,
and think that there must be ways to give
back what you gave.
But the sentence stands. We never found
words in which we could both live.

Song for a Tourist

When upon this fabled beach
you in nightmare rise to watch
twilit lives enact their fate

and the stars eliminate
oiled civility and touch
(make no lyric memories)

passion's faggot where it lies,
while the blood-dark ocean cries
'Walk softly, danger, danger!'

Make no lyric memories.
Stranger, these are Siren Isles.
Make no lyric memories

stranger, stranger, stranger!

Jan Carew

The Dreamtime Lives Again

Aubrey, you splashed the sun in my face
made sunlight dance out of canvas-dreams
Cockatoos, Harpy Eagles, Kiskadees,
Hoatzins, Maams, King Vultures, Blue Sackees
rainbowed landscapes of your mind's eye.
You awakened Maridowa from a dreamless sleep
sent her on a walk-about from green hills of home
down the Moruka, the Bara-Bara, the Biara,
the Kaituma, to Hosororo of green mysteries
where Carib Piaimen
live dreamtime eternity to seasons
astride secret itabus
of Children of the Sun again.
Maridowa's long canoe, sleek as a serpent,
parted tides of sorrow at Waini's estuary
and entering the amber-tinted sea
raced white horses
across sun-spangled esplanades
of wind and roaring surf
until Paria calmed the wind's temper
and through the Bocas her long canoe sped
racing emerald islands
between seasons of Hurrican.
Hurrican watched with his eye of silence
in his right hand he wielded
the Thunder-Axe
in his left
the Lightning-Eel.
Maridowa, homing her long canoe
on black and white sands of Camerhone
skipped across island stepping-stones

with Wendigo feet
Kanaima watched malevolently
but could not reach her with his rage
Maridowa walked to Guanahani
where Christobal Colon
Sea-horseman of Apocalypse
was discovered by gentle Tainos
before oblivion shrouded them
in holocausts of hate.
Maridowa, Mother of the Hills,
giant-strided it across twenty thousand cays
to the Peninsula of flowers
and Chicoria
of vanished sons and daughters
of the Shaking Earth
Aubrey, now that you've gone
to walk amongst the stars
crimes of the conquistadores
can no longer be secreted away
in archives of ocean spray
on tourist beaches.
Maridowa's walking again
with Wendigo feet
Hurrican's rage can no longer be caged.
Quetzal birds are winging their way
to Temples of the Sun again
Souls of those who died
to make the earth a better place
rainbow skies with butterflies again
Plumed serpents are slithering
inside Pyramids of life
The heritage is safe.

Tiho, The Carib

The first time I saw the sea
I did not know
it was not green like parrots
or rainbowed like macaws' wings.
The first time the sea spoke to me
it sounded different
from trees
and rivers,
my mother's singing or
wind combing the hair
of tall savannah grass.
The first time I touched the sea
it licked my feet
with a rough tongue
like an ocelot's
and wind sang to me:
wide the world wide, boy,
wide and deep!
Wide the world wide, boy,
wider than the heart can reach,
wide the world wide, boy!

Martin Carter

Bitter Wood

Here be dragons, and bitter
cups made of wood; and the hooves
of horses where they should not
sound. Yet on the roofs of houses
walk the carpenters, as once did
cartographers on the spoil
of splendid maps. Here is where
I am, in a great geometry, between
a raft of ants and the green sight
of the freedom of a tree, made
of that same bitter wood.

A Mouth Is Always Muzzled

In the premises of the tongue
dwells the anarchy of the ear;
in the chaos of the vision
resolution of the purpose.

And would shout it out differently
if it could be sounded plain;
But a mouth is always muzzled
by the food it eats to live.

Rain was the cause of roofs.
Birth was the cause of beds.
But life is the question asking
what is the way to die.

After One Year

After today, how shall I speak with you?
Those miseries I know you cultivate
are mine as well as yours, or do you think
the impartial bullock cares whose land is ploughed?

I know this city much as well as you do,
the ways leading to brothels and those dooms
dwelling in them, as in our lives they dwell.
So jail me quickly, clang the illiterate door
if freedon writes no happier alphabet.

Old hanging ground is still green playing field.
Smooth cemetery proud garden of tall flowers.
But in your secret gables real bats fly
mocking great dreams that give the soul no peace,
and everywhere wrong deeds are being done.

Rude citizen! think you I do not know
that love is stammered, hate is shouted out
in every human city in this world?
Men murder men, as men must murder men,
to build their shining governments of the damned.

Childhood of a Voice

The light oppresses and the darkness frees
a man like me, who never cared at all:
Imagine it, the childhood of a voice
and voice of childhood telling me my name.

But if only the rain would fall,
and the sky we have not seen so long
come blue again.

The familiar white street
is tired of always running east.
The sky, of always arching over.
The tree, of always reaching up.

Even the round earth is tired of being round
and spinning round the sun.

In a Small City at Dusk

In a small city at dusk
it is difficult to distinguish
bird from bat. Both fly fast:
one away from the dark
and one toward the dark.
The bird to a nest in the tree
The bat to a feast in its branches.

Stranger to each other they seek
planted by beak or claw or hand
the same tree that grows out of the great soil.
And I know, even before I came to live here,
before the city had so many houses
dusk did the same to bird and bat and does
the same to man.

Bent

On the street, the sun
rages. The bent back of
an old woman resurrects
the brimmed bucket of this world's

light and insupportable
agony. A damage of years.

Her bent back, time's bad
step, and the creeping out
is ash; is the crushed cloud
of an incredible want.

The last time I saw her
she was far more truthful
that the damage of the years
carried on her back. The
sky, blue and ever,
imitates her. Bent.

Being Always

Being, always to arrange
myself in the world, and the world
in myself, I try to do both. How
both are done is difficult. Why,
I have to ask, do I have to
arrange anything when every
thing is already arranged
by love's and death's inscrutable
laws, mortal judiciary, time's
doll house of replaceable heads,
arms and legs? In another
house, not time's, time itself arranges
mine and the world's replacement.

Brian Chan

Paradise

These islands we people
as ghosts, no matter how
rooted our crops, cities
and walls against the sea
that lets us these altars
of our masochistic
leaf-passion for the wind
coming to rape our trees
or over the sea's edge
flinging our fishing boats
like shadows, like black leaves.

How to Organise a Successful Small Business

Wise up, Pablito. Each frame looks too
different from the next: don't admit
to being so many men. Settle
for this: a corner where no one else
has thought of perching, repeat and refine one
splash till it tastes like The Man Himself.
Erase the orange eyes, the green tongue,
change that blue fist into a purple green palm.
There are banks, medals, haloes, other lives.

Faustin Charles

Letters from Home

1

The wind writes to me
Of a storm brewing in the Caribbean,
Raging waters and breaking mountains
Into dust.
I see heads rolling in the mid-day heat,
Eyes blinded by the sting of scorpion's blood,
I hear screams between the lines of blazing fire,
And Grenada choking in the eagle's throat.
The wind's pen trembles in expectancy,
Leaves bursting into tears:
A greedy giant is eating the Caribbean.

2

The sun sends me wires of blue rain,
Horizons littered with corpses;
Red ants gnawing a poem to the bone
Building an ant-hill of broken bones;
Through the tortured light, the islands crash,
Uprooting their dreams in a mirage of wealth.
In trying to become what we are not,
We are losing the reality of what we are.
Words travelling the Atlantic
Whistling drum-calls blading troubled waters
Communing with soothsayers and smugglers.
The sun's postscript ponders
Lost hopes and regrets
Knotted on a clothes-line.

LeRoy Clarke

Soucouyant

> *Death herself,*
> *the chief celebrant,*
> *in a cloud of incense,*
> *paring her fingernails . . .*
> CHRISTOPHER OKIGBO

For the Vampires of the Caribbean

. . . their first hours wore nice costumes.
        These bandages hide our sores.

land is up, worth twenty dollars per sq. foot
        our hands are shells of hot air.

two, three, four cars, eat drink your ass up.
        under this imported silk, my dirty drawers.

the streets coil about him like dark constrictors.
        my house is empty my love, come home.

those who represent us are so handsomely dressed.
        we were taught, a star is a star, let's follow.

and we may have one, maybe no children . . .
        gaze on my breasts of stoned butterflies.

Perched there on an awning
of concrete and leaves of steel,
among flags and anthems of spiders,
among pledges, among deeds and manifestos . .

the soucouyant, her eyes
a million flies, wide and sharp. .

among broken knives and smoking pistols
among stain and glitter of costumes
of clouds, of armies and police,
among salutes and commendations . .

the soucouyant, her eyes
a million flies, wide and sharp . .

among the hot hollows . . along the new
tarmacs . . in the noise . . in the dust . .
leading her hogs to the cliffs . . .

the soucouyant perched, her eyes
a million flies wide and sharp overlooking . . .

the blood turned beggar cries like a lamb
on this landscape of skulls laid drunk
and staggers in piss, lifts its arms
to salvage fiber from smoke . .

and heard salt quarrels of gulls,
ashanti necks, headless on an only leg,
on a hope of elongated shadow, where
crabs hurry with secrets into silence . . .

the soucouyant, perched, her eyes
a million flies wide and sharp.

attending, replete as worms, crawling
into bone and all, her ministrants
tumble success on each other,
wallow bile for bile.

teeth, wildpine displayed as orchids
plunge with the spirit of an adze, deep,
                              deeper into wood.

chop, chopping-up man and mountain
chop, chopping-up breasts and laughter
chop-butterflies, ferns and eyes
chop-up navels and thighs
chop-up hands and desires
chop-up dreams and food
chop-up nests and fires
chop-up fish and bread
                    and respect for books and art
                    and scorpions and worms
                    and earth and sky
                    and sounds of birds
                    and wind and water
                    rain . . and my whistling.

licking her gums over bones of school,
of church, of prison, of star, entering
a pore, turning turning
each skin to bone to skin
to flesh turning, entering
turning entering to turn flesh
to bone to soul of flame of sin.

the soucouyant, her eyes a million flies
wide and sharp, in her perch,
vomits her roll
of doctors and lawyers
her teachers, pets and pains
underwriters . . . and you
may-invent-any-man here . . .
                              Soucouyant . . soucouyant.

Merle Collins

Because the Dawn Breaks

We speak
because
when the rain falls
in the mountains
the river slowly swells

Comes rushing down
over boulders
across roads
crumbling bridges
that would hold their power
against its force

We speak
for the same reason
that
the thunder frightens the child
that
the lightning startles the tree

We do not speak
to defy your tenets
though we do
or upset your plans
even though we do
or to tumble
your towers of babel
we speak
in spite of the fact
that we do

We speak
because
your plan
is not our plan
our plan
we speak because we dream
because
our dreams
are not of living in pig pens
in any other body's
backyard
not of
catching crumbs from tables
not of crawling forever
along the everlasting ant-line
to veer away in quick detour
when the elephant's foot
crashes down
not of having to turn back
when the smell of death
assails our senses
not of striving forever
to catch the image of your Gods
within our creation

We speak
for the same reason
that
the flowers bloom
that the sun sets
that the fruit ripens

because temples built
to honour myths
must crumble
as the dawn breaks

there is nothing you can do
about your feeble bridges
when the rain falls
in the mountains
and swells the flow of rivers

We speak
not to agitate you
but in spite of your agitation
because
we are workers
peasants
leaders
you see
and were not born
to be your vassals

Trapped

Butterfly
trapped in a mould
of molten steel
wings open
poised for flight
caught by more
than the matter seen
wish I knew where history been
wish I knew
where they make the fire
that melt the steel
that make the prison
to hold the butterfly
that spirits made

Christine Craig

City Blues

Estelle irons khaki and navy
blue for school tomorrow.
Need a school shoes for Rosie.
A which part Sam gone. Dem
so sweet when dem a hunt you
down an swift as chicken hawk
fe gone when dem get you.
Seem like gone is a word
fe spell wid a **m** an a **a**
an a **n**.

Estelle fights her way in
the mini-bus, uptown to look
a work. No work. Me can sew
you know mam. No work. Me can
bake and cook and clean floor
till you see you face inna it.
No work. Estelle with housekeeping
skills and no house to keep,
only empty cupboards, cold stove
and children soon reach home
hungry. Swallow you pride girl
go see you sister Norma.
You know say she a go harass
you soul case but blood
thicker dan water. Mornin,
Norma, how you keeping?

Norma is keeping an office job
and church on Sunday looking
for a fine up-right man. Norma
is studying books for night
school and every day planning
how to move up, how to talk
good so nobody will know seh
is Jones Town she coming from.
What happen Estelle, you see
me name bank? When you a lie down
wid different man you don't tink
bout how you a go manage.

Estelle, star of heartbreak,
prefers learning the no job
pavements step by step, edging
past the mad sculptor who creates
with boxes and signs, with old shoes
and rags carefully shaped round
a leafless tree. Walking home
with dollar cornmeal and Marley
catching at the edge of her mind
who feels it knows it Lord.

Weep, weep for us women on the streets
of Kingston. Weep for our children
hungry, angry in this town that blooms
large houses, smooth lawns where other
children play computer games and plan
the next trip to Miami.
Weep but also watch Estelle, dark star
in an anguished sky. No poem, no
politics, no church, no way to close
this wound only an endless searching,
seeking to meet ourselves,
greet ourselves, honourably.

Cyril Dabydeen

The Husband

After a week
In the town's brothel
He came home
Bringing Shamin, the town whore
With him

His fat wife (she was once beautiful
With fair skin)
Sat in the kitchen and grumbled
By herself

I, one of the villagers, gossiped
Like the rest
While he remained
In the bedroom upstairs
In the house built
On stilts

His wife knew there
Was nothing she could do
But wait until his passion
Was sated
      —with a bottle of rum

She muttered about leaving him
But she never really did—
    'It was bound to happen that way,'
I heard her once say
    to her children

Afterwards he played
    the mandolin beautifully–
His wife laughed
    all by herself

Dubious Foreigner

As there is no doubt
    where I come from

I answer to all the mistrust
    you let out
        onto myself

A dollar value citizenship card
    bulges out
        against my hide of skin

I repeat history
    to myself
        once in a while–

my feet spread out
    against a liana sun
        –swinging against the horizon

belching out the past
    with Asia & Africa
        in my ears

Next, iridescent & emerald
    as the waves
        I acknowledge the pattern

answering to myself
    in Canada—
        with crabgrass

on snowy virginal
    ground

Patriot

I remind myself that I am
tropical to the bones
I blend with a temperate
carapace
hard lines form
across my face
I am anxious to make Canada
meet in me
I make designs
all across
the snow

David Dabydeen

Catching Crabs

Ruby and me stalking savannah
Crab season with cutlass and sack like big folk.
Hiding behind stones or clumps of bush
Crabs locked knee-deep in mud mating
And Ruby, seven years old feeling strange at the sex
And me horrified to pick them up
Plunge them into the darkness of bag.
So all day we scout to catch the lonesome ones
Who don't mind cooking because they got no prospect
Of family, and squelching through the mud,
Cutlass clearing bush at our feet,
We come home tired slow, weighed down with plenty
Which Ma throw live into boiling pot piece-piece.
Tonight we'll have one big happy curry feed,
We'll test out who teeth and jaw strongest
Who will grow up to be the biggest
Or who will make most terrible cannibal.

We leave behind a mess of bones and shell
And come to England and America
Where Ruby hustles in a New York tenement
And me writing poetry at Cambridge,
Death long catch Ma, the house boarded up
Breeding wasps, woodlice in its dark-sack belly:
I am afraid to walk through weed yard,
Reach the door, prise open, look,
In case the pot still bubbles magical
On the fireside, and I see Ma

Working a ladle, slow –
Limbed, crustacean-old, alone,
In case the woodsmoke and curry steam
Burn my child-eye and make it cry.

Coolie Mother

Jasmattie live in bruk –
Down hut big like Bata shoe-box,
Beat clothes, weed yard, chop wood, feed fowl
For this body and that body and every blasted body,
Fetch water, all day fetch water like if the whole –
Whole slow-flowing Canje river God create
Just for *she* one own bucket.

Till she foot-bottom crack and she hand cut-up
And curse swarm from she mouth like red-ants
And she cough blood on the ground but mash it in:
Because Jasmattie heart hard, she mind set hard.

To hustle save she one-one slow penny,
Because one-one dutty* make dam cross the Canje
And she son Harilall *got* to go school in Georgetown,
Must wear clean starch pants, or they go laugh at he,
Strap leather on he foot, and he *must* read book,
Learn talk proper, take exam, go to England university,
Not turn out like he rum-sucker chamar† dadee.

*dutty: piece of earth
† chamar: low-caste

Coolie Son

(The Toilet Attendant Writes Home)

Taana boy, how you do?
How Shanti stay? And Sukhoo?
Mosquito still a-bite all-you?
Juncha dead true-true?
Mala bruk-foot set?
Food deh foh eat yet?

Englan nice, snow and dem ting,
A land dey say fit for a king,
Iceapple plenty on de tree and bird a-sing –
Is de beginning of what dey call 'The Spring'.

And I eating enough for all a-we
And reading book bad-bad.

But is what make Matam wife fall sick
And Sonnel cow suck dry wid tick?

Soon, I go turn lawya or dacta,
But, just now, passage money run out
So I tek lil wuk –
I is a Deputy Sanitary Inspecta,
Big-big office, boy! Tie round me neck!
Brand new uniform, one big bunch keys!
If Ma can see me now how she go please. . . .

Miranda

His black bony peasant body
Stalk of blighted cane
In dry earth.

I will blot out the tyrant sun
Cleanse you in the raincloud of my body
In the secrecy of night set you supple and erect.

And wiped him with the moist cloth of her tongue
Like a new mother licking clean its calf
And hugged milk from her breast to his cracked mouth.

That when he woke he cried to dream again
Of the scent of her maternity
The dream of the moon of her deep spacious eye.

Sea-blue and bountiful
Beyond supplication or conquest
A frail slave vessel wracked upon a mere pebble of her promise.

And the sun resumed its cruelty
And the sun shook with imperial glee
At the fantasy.

Fred D'Aguiar

Mama Dot's Treatise

Mosquitoes
Are the fattest
Inhabitants
Of this republic.

They suck our blood
From the cradle
And flaunt it
Like a fat wallet.

They form dark
Haloes; we spend
Our outdoors
Dodging sainthood.

They force us
Into an all-night
Purdah of nets
Against them.

O to stop them
Milking us
Till we are bait
For worms;

Worms that don't
Know which way
To turn and will
Inherit the earth.

Airy Hall's Exits

Salt over the shoulder
Or a trip curtailed,
On account of the black cat
That crossed your path.

Last rites for the sick
In a house a crow
Overflew or preened itself on
And cawed, cawed, cawed.

A black dress, the gift
From a relative you've never seen,
For the funeral of a friend
You never imagined could die.

The dream you fall in,
Waking seconds before you land,
Your heart backfiring; the dream
You one day fail to wake from.

The Cow Perseverance

I

Here I am writing you on old newspaper against a tide of print,
In the regular spaces between lines (there are no more trees).
I've turned it upside-down to widen the gap bordering sense and
　　nonsense,
For what I must say might very well sound as if it were topsy-
　　turvy.
I put myself in your shoes (unable to recall when I last set eyes on
　　a pair).

You read everything twice, then to be doubly sure, aloud,
Testing their soundness: *we wash cow's dung for its grain*,
And I feel your stomach turn; it's not much unlike collecting it for
    fuel,
Or mixed with clay to daub cracks in our shelters and renew
    door-mounds
That free us of rain, insects and spirits. They no longer drop the
    milk
We let them live for; their nights spent indoors for safe keep,
Their days tethered to a nearby post. People eye them so, they are
    fast
Becoming our cross; you'd think they'd fallen out of the sky.

II

Hunger has filled them with what I can only call compassion.
Such bulbous, watery eyes blame us for the lack of grass and
    worse,
Expect us to do something; tails that held the edge of windscreen
    wipers
In better days, swishing the merest irritant, a feather's even,
Let flies congregate until the stretched, pockmarked hide is them.
That's why, when you asked how things were, I didn't have to
    look far.
I thought, *Let the cow explain, its leathery tongue has run this
    geography
Many times over*; how milk turns, unseen, all at once, so lush
    pastures
Threw up savannahs. The storms are pure dust or deep inside the
    rowdiest
Among us, virtually dead and rowdy because they know it,
    they're not sure
What else to do. You fathom why, when a cow croons, we offer it
What we can't as a bribe for it to stop: *silence is perseverance*.

III

We watch its wait on meagre haunches, ruminating on what must be
Imperishable leather, some secret mantra, our dear buddha, for the miracle
We need; and us, with nowhere to turn, find we believe. God knows
It's a case of choosing which pot-hole in the road to ride; knowing
We export the asphalt that could fill them; knowing too the one thing
We make these days that is expressly ours is whipped in malarial water
And forced down our throats for daring to open our mouths.
Give us the cow's complicity anyday: its perfect art of being left
In peace; its till-now effortless conversion of chewy grass to milk;
And its daft hoof-print, ignored for so long though clearly trespassing.
Then and then alone, we too can jump over the moon, without bloodshed.
Its raised-head and craned-neck attempt to furnish an exact account
Is a tale you and I are bound to finish, in flesh or spirit.

Mahadai Das

Horses

All the pink-coloured horses are coming in.
They gallop in from the sunset, hearts
beating like a drum.

Unbridled, they canter,
Flushed. Approaching twilight.
Behind, Sun is a blaze of metal
Sinking into the sea.

Where are the golden horsemen?
They too are drowning.
They will rise from the Sea tomorrow.
Their dust will rise up from the east.

Meanwhile, the horses come in,
last troops in the twilight,
with their hoofs of steel, their wild manes.
The drums from the Amazon are thundering and,
breasty women are blowing into the fire.

The children are petulant, sucking their thumbs
with outcast expressions.
It is suppertime and their stomachs are groaning.

But outside the hut, the men
are hammering the goatskin drums with their fingers.
They wait for the horses to come in.

The Growing Tip

They sought the 'growing tip of poetry,'
its first frail-green shoots
on which to 'ooh' and 'aah'.

They assumed a garden: English roses,
palms of victory high-raised
on a history of thorns, thick
hedges, neatly-trimmed.

They assumed a gardener:
a 'Being There' type seeding
and nurturing and coaxing gardening's
lengthy process from seed to flower;
finally, beaming with his gloating,
false pride of parenthood.

They assumed a house
to which the garden attached,
a black leech of thirst upon
an oasis of blood; a benevolent master,
gentle mistress, mischievous, annoying
harmless children.

Perhaps they assumed a car or two,
a dog, a cat, a singing canary
hanging by its wiry prison on the porch;
a jolly postman, a friendly milkman,
an ever-so-often handyman.

What she sent reminded no one of a garden:
pieces of skin, a handful of hair, broken
teeth, bits of glass – an iron chest, rusty, grim. . .

She told of jungles, of suppers of snakes
and monkeys; of bills evaded by a change-of-address;
of late payments as a matter of principle;
of forgetting genres of old people, babies
and children; of a living-for-oneself philosophy
which led one, like a modern-day Christ
to bear his cross to the Lonely Hill of the Gallows.

Oh she had things that grew —
horns and tails, arms of different lengths,
automatic fangs near bureaucrats, a tail,
(a bit of bother when she wore a dress);
aunts whose heads she preserved in bottles
of pickles on a shelf, a father stoned
by a proliferation of Oedipal daughters

'Aiee!' they cried, 'What a monster!'
'This is not a plant!' said the editor-chief.
'It's not a tree!' cried another.

'It's not a rosebush!' (they) cried in unison.
'Not a weed!' a shy one piped at last.

A plant from another planet?

Not a plant?

Even as they peeled off postage-stamps,
horns grew right out of each ear!

When they picked SASE out
from its envelope, a tail uncoiled,
(it caused quite a shriek!)

'My God! It grows,   it grows,   it grows!'

As they watched,

        in high shock,

from every tip,

        it continued to grow.

Learner

I am the great learner.
I devour the apple but before that,
I halve then quarter
and eighth it.

I am a baby feeding on mashed yams.
I discover red apples and green ones,
small apples, large ones. Romanos.
Granny Smiths.

I have eaten them.
Flame in the gut. Like a Chinese dragon,
I hold horses I drive and I breathe fire.
Adam and Eve in one, I am in a garden
Eating. Breathing.
There are raspberries too, and bananas.
The banana-man sells me some.

I, oriental fire-dragon, mother Kali
in China, wrap snakes around my neck and
I the fruits, belching out ribbons of fire
into the snow-white prison to which I am
Relegated.
Bars are white hot iron.
Books encased in cartoons stand low
against the bars.

The Leaf in his Ear

For Charlie

Left, the golden leaf bears from his ear.
At eighteen, Bushman fighting to control diamonds
in his glass head. The waters of the river
swirl by.

I and I, Rastaman, with knotty India hair, has long ago, ceased.
The good Lord swallowed him up.
Into Guiana forests. North-west.
Dogs bark and howl.
In this first of May day, the Almighty is Rain,
voices, wind in banana suckers.

Gloria Escoffery

Mother Jackson Murders the Moon

Mother Jackson
sees the moon coming at her
and slams the door of her shack
so hard
the tin louvers shudder with eagerness
to let the moon in.
If she should cry for help
the dog would skin his teeth at her,
the cat would hoist his tail
and pin the moonlit sky
to the gutter;
the neighbours would maybe
douse her in chicken's blood
and hang her skin to dry
on the packy tree.
Mother Jackson
swallows her bile and sprinkles oil
from the kitchen bitch
on her ragged mattress.
Then she lights a firestick and waits
for the moon to come in and take her.

After the Fall

Swordscape, tombscape, flame ploughed
Where the old man gilt fingered reads, born; died
Needs must in between have suffered, lied
Sighing at the milk spill hushing.
Now herself fallen

Silent as thin piped water
As lined on blanched stones pure
To her own epitaph a whisper
To the young signpainter, coon capped.
A shadow, to ginger farmers
A fragrance of nutmeg.

Let the young shout,
My dog, my house, my wife,
Pale water carriers in the land's dawn
Before the fall.

Tricks of the Trade

A few quick drying globs of gold acrylic,
said one artist to another,
will do the trick.
But the other stolidly went on
tricking out the surface with glazes
in oils so he had to wait following
each move he made one whole week to decide
what next; and by then
his own undercover agent upstairs
had sent him to the window to reconsider
the skin of the land, usually bush green to
                                most witnesses
but now a sort of drought-parched brown.
And colour climbed up to peep
through the artist's eyes and his landscape
blossomed in unlisted off-
emeralds and ochres with just a tinge
of sun burnt sienna; revealing that
here in the tropics all the seasons are
underfoot all the year round.

John Figueroa

Epitaph

The old man is gone
>   Him ded, sah, him ded!
(Where are the frigate birds?)

Absent from Jonkunoo Lounge,
Someone will miss him from
The Caribe Bar – but only long
After.
>   Him ded, sah, him ded!

In Santiago de los Caballeros
(O Spanish men on horses!)
They will remember when
It is too late how lively he
Could be.
>   Him ded, sah; se murio.
But Tavern on the Green
Will dance, and Tower Isle
And Myrtle Bank, so stupidly
Demolished.
>   (Him done ded, sah)
And wherever for a moment or
A night he used to cast the spell
Against death with dancing –
A spell that works and does
Not work.
>   (Him ded, sah, him ded!)
A spell that did not last.

The frigate birds have soared away.
The hurricane clouds have left
The skies clean blue;
And in the silence he has danced
Away, away, across the bar.

      Him no ded, sah?

This tree my time keeper

This tree my time keeper
is brown with berries now

When last I looked it had
no leaves, was stiff and white
with frost.

Now green leaves and brown berries toss,
toss and bob in the whipping wind.

It is not Spring beyond the horizon
that the bucking boat is heading for,

'It is not Spring with its false hopes,
it is not Spring,' says my time keeper,

'but bitter berries, bitter and brown
and full of wisdom.'

Only in hard winters, they tell me
will the birds touch these berries.

Honor Ford-Smith

Lala: The Dressmaker

Across from Chang's Green Emporium,
at Halfway Tree, near the fish fry sidewalk
where the men now sit to play at winning
crown and anchor – the dress shop circled her.
Inch measure of her life's scramble –
mountain range of chequered scraps
scent of fabric satin and taffeta –
on the wheels of the foot machines
tread-treading on the raw edges of
parties, teas and mothers' union's socials,
she was drawn into town, moving yard
by yard on the trains of bridal gowns,
fashioning a living from these things.
There was nothing else to do.

The rack of finished dresses, hanging, linings out,
concealed the beadwork her fingers were known for.
(A bald pink mannequin stood in the window –
Issa's had made them necessary.)
She, seated behind the children's magic mahogany
and glass case cargo of the trade's beads, buttons,
zippers, a bangle, pencil, candle – even fruit,
finished collars. The firm fat of her hands
dissolved by time into a skein of thin brown linen.
One son. No husband. In silence
she stitched the distant canefield's cotton trees,
her shame-me-lady face half hidden by the shoulder length
crisp straightened hair. Occasionally, laughter
like a sluice gate crinkled the black black eyes.

*   *   *

Once, before, in the town's taboo, Mohammed's
secret raft of tissue paper and bamboo stood among the
indentured ready to float back to him,
the Indian women chanting
'Allah man say husseh'
She earned her name Lala mingling with the chant
then
breaking, climbing, tearing at the women's work
to see the forbidden centre of the thing.

And afterwards, the dry red heat of malaria,
journeying, fighting, fighting through the hot cloth
covering a sea of seaweed, to the place where
years later, behind the hidden patterns in the stripped
backroom of the shop, between rough walls
across the naked cedar table, she gambled on futures,
staring into the muddled darjeeling leaves
calling the good fortunes of the women to life.

*   *   *

When Lala died
in the backroom of the shop
the girlchildren she had clothed,
whose futures she chose from those cupped in her hand
unpicked the beaded dresses to find what she hid
stitched in the lining.
They put the beads in the locks of their hair
their needles flashing (dangerous and quick)
collecting the light
opening
opening
their laughter strikes the centre of the clock
at Halfway Tree and the flames of the alleys
lick the rotten wooden walls.

Aux Leon . . . Women

Before the sunlight
splits the dry rock
their eyes open
on coarse board walls and
guttered
government
land

mind set begins
with stumbling over
a sleeping child
an animal immobile

'catch up the fire/ scrape and grate the cassava/ carry the water
(uphill)/ boil the tea/ the toloma/ beat the castor oil seeds/
wash clothes/ nurse baby/ soothe old lady/ weed garden/ chop
banana/ load banana/ carry it down the stony road/
Un cadeau pour Monsieur Guise'
la lin coowee, coowee
la solei joo baway
(the moon runs
it runs
till the sun
catches it)
'how much are the bananas today/ the housewife said
unbuttoning her coat/ laying down her string bag in the
Islington shop/ hurry up there/ don't have all day/ she added
himself will be home soon and the tea not ready/ nothing
changes/ only the prices rise/ Gimme a dozen a them/ bruised
lot you got here today/'
la lin coowee, coowee
la solei joo baway
(the moon runs
it runs

till the sun
catches it)
scrape/ boil/ beat
'sleep baby sleep
father working far away
he give me something i take it
he give me nothing   i take it'
Aux Leon women
This morning
when the sunlight strikes
the rock
Let us sweep that old yard clean.
Let us beat our quarrels into one voice
with the rhythm of the hardwood pestle.
Let us light our fires on this hillside
so all the islands will see
this labour is not free.
Let us burn the sweet wood
for its scent will fill the nostrils
of the blind and deaf.

listen
(la solei coowee coowee
la lin joo baway)
The stroke of a cutlass in water has no meaning
(la solei coowee coowee
la lin joo baway)
Listen, a song –
a song is beginning
right here
among us

Aux Leon is a small community in Saint Lucia, situated near Dennery on the
eastern side of the island and created by squatters on the high and rocky backlands
of an old estate.

Anson Gonzalez

Gasparillo Remembered

rushed out when the bullock carts
laden with succulent stalks passed

saw them change the crops
to iron hard hybrids that broke teeth

no more joy when we pulled our prizes
from passing carts or rare farm-als

collected the arrow pollen
for so many restful pillows
each year's end and beginning

and fed free cane stalk fodder
to my hungry animals

for five months annually friends were tired
with toil from labours in field and factory

no liming now except Saturday nights
for the next seven months precarious survival

hustling hanging around jobhunting

but among the hustle and road dangers
the heat, scarred skin and cane soot

the sugared wallet bulged on payday

today I know no one by name
in the canefield or sugar factory

the leading cane-cutter sputters
in his grey suited parliamentary postures

more sophisticated than I or they
or any other actor could hope to be

and the cane arrows point upward
a magnificent tourist brochure
along the newly repaired highway

and using foam for pillows now
I avoid sugar as much as possible
and know none by name in field or factory

First Friday Bell

. . . in memory of Mama who died suffering

The first Friday bell shatters the morning
and shuffling feet respond to the call

your dim, grey shape joins the procession
again pulling a dozen wagons which

are the churches you used to hurry to
filled with plaster saints and incantations,

you treasured them and kept bright shiny
beads while at death's door you lay pain wracked

and tortured, eaten away by some greedy
demon, your flesh falling off and melting

into air; and I could only watch you
mumble, eating your pain to spare me

no church no god seemed to help you and I
watched you with dread and admiration and

love and hate. Yes, hate! I hated your
suffering like Job or some dumb animal

there with nerves aquiver and sunken eyes
and painful submission to your loving

Maker. How I wished to relieve you but
you were content to bite your teeth and hold

back the bitter tears while I looked helplessly
and admired you, pitied you, and loved you

and as the first Friday bell rings, I hear
your footsteps join the band of faithful and

your lips fluttering as you pass the beads
and drag your wagon-churches and I weep

Little Rosebud Girl

soon to bloom
in splendour
then
to
wither
and
f
a
d
e

Lorna Goodison

Keith Jarrett – Rainmaker

Piano man
my roots are african
I dwell in the centre of the sun.
I am used to its warmth
I am used to its heat
I am seared by its vengeance
(it has a vengeful streak)

So my prayers are usually
for rain.
My people are farmers
and artists
and sometimes the lines
blur
so a painting becomes a
december of sorrel
a carving heaps like a yam hill
or a song of redemption wings
like the petals of resurrection
lilies – all these require rain.
So this sunday
when my walk misses
my son's balance on my hips
I'll be alright if you pull down
for me
waterfalls of rain.
I never thought a piano
could divine
but I'm hearing you this morning
and right on time
its drizzling now

I'll open the curtains and
watch the lightning conduct
your hands.

Guinea Woman

Great grandmother
was a guinea woman
wide eyes turning
the corners of her face
could see behind her
her cheeks dusted with
a fine rash of jet-bead warts
that itched when the rain set up.

Great grandmother's waistline
the span of a headman's hand
slender and tall like a cane stalk
with a guinea woman's antelope-quick walk
and when she paused
her gaze would look to sea
her profile fine like some obverse impression
on a guinea coin from royal memory.

It seems her fate was anchored
in the unfathomable sea
for great grandmother caught the eye of a sailor
whose ship sailed without him from Lucea harbour.
Great grandmother's royal scent of
cinnamon and escallions
drew the sailor up the straits of Africa,
the evidence my blue-eyed grandmother
the first Mulatta
taken into backra's household

and covered with his name.
They forbade great grandmother's
guinea woman presence
they washed away her scent of
cinnamon and escallions
controlled the child's antelope walk
and called her uprisings rebellions.

But, great grandmother
I see your features blood dark
appearing
in the children of each new
breeding
the high yellow brown
is darkening down.
Listen, children
it's great grandmother's turn.

Gleanings

Often, it's a field at dark
where the hooded bowed outcasts
go, after the reapers have passed
collecting then, the gleanings.

Sometimes after the harvest is in
and the fields are lying spent
they still move in twilight foraging
for the seeds the birds have missed.

(What a hard time the post-harvest is!)

We glean outside the system
our candidate did not win.
We glean outside our father's yard
the stewards are self serving.

We glean outside the temples of fullness
for charity dropped careless
from full sheaves above.
It is time to come into the kingdom.

Jean Goulbourne

This is the Place Where . . .

This here is the place
where
the potholes sink in the mud
where
water rise from the gutter
and grins at the M.P.
where the sun goes down
and never rise,

Where the dog
eat the garbage so clean
the poor stomach in pain . . .

Where the minibus man
knock the badwords so loud
it louder than Yellowman singing.

Where the moon rise and smile
at the man with the trigger
in his pants . . .

Where Sunday morning
it so holy, church full
and de parson preach
and de children still,

Till Monday morning when,

This here is the place where . . .

One Acre

Child
With ancient face
Sits
upon the immortal stone
Thatch hat
on withered head
Rags
upon a puny body
Club feet
touches the ground
waiting . . .

Father
Wipes the sweat
from
a black face
Fingers
falling yam vines
Finds
the hoe handle
sighs . . .

One acre
of worms
a lifetime
of toil.

Cecil Gray

The Misses Norman

The Misses Norman lived on Marine Square
just as you turn from Broadway at the corner
where now a granite bank shines like new coins;
two short white matrons that I remember
like Lord's Prayers on a rosary that joins
a knotted childhood to their acts of care.

To my young mind it seemed a threatening place.
You pierced the wooden gate through its small door
and stepped into a dimness armed with plants,
cringed up the half-gloom to the upper floor
and called good morning nervous in your pants.
But there you spoke with goodness face to face.

With thanks now rising in me like a lake
an image flashes fresh as yesterday:
a slippered sister in Edwardian dress
shuffling to hear each stanza of distress,
bribing the waiting teeth of reefs away.
It is a bonding that time cannot break.

The lifeguards of this heaving world are rare,
the sinking swimmers thick as August rain.
But one whose feet touched safety when that pair
of spinsters anchored themselves to pain
that was not theirs attempts a line of praise
in words like them, as faithful and as plain.

Funeral Service

The little church was glowing
with mid-morning sun. Light
took possession of its pointed
windows. But countenances
were drawn with solemn lines
enacting sorrow for the dead.
The mauve casket was the hub.
Tongues of candles spluttered
then burned straight to aim
their invocations. Friends
spoke whispering their nods
like sly adolescents. Gowned
clerics ministered the slide
of the bright castors carrying
the bier with puffs of incense,
threnodies and prayer. Their
shrewd words sealed a covenant
giving the dead reward. The
promise shone with comfort
down the aisle.

          The rites went on.
But I was mourning only for myself
and for a death inside. Demise
of hope needs some other sign
to ease its burial when the end
has come. There should be rituals
to soften thuds that pound upon
a coffin closed and lowered
when years have had their run.

The organ piped
a coda shrill and high, a dirge
that activated in my thoughts
a lesson of its own: that some
things do not ripen over time
but burst with instant passion
or expire. Nurtured appreciation
has no flame and love that grows
from tutoring is a dud without
much worth. It was a lesson
I had waited for. It came
and brought me burial clothes
to wear. The hymn that soothed
through that long bonding
had pulled the stops to pour
into my ear the words that broke
free from a hidden sepulcre.
They told who made excitement
burn her with its charge.
All I could have would never
come to that.

          I turned
and left the church. The bier,
the grave, the last delusion,
placed within its box.

A. L. Hendriks

Jamaican Small Gal

Small gal, Jamaican, she came to me,
Said: 'Lissen mi, Baas; Look what wi see!
Hard time dah ketch wi, eh Missa D?
What wi to do now? Fah Gawd mek us free.
Mi come from country, mi Pappa have grung,
'im plant out one canepiece when mi was young
But den 'im tek sick, spit blood from 'im lung,
So mi get up an' leave an' come into tung.
But Kingston is madness mi cyan unnderstan'.
How come dem have swim-pool pan good growin' lan'?
An' golf-course an' big house, w'ile poor nayga man
Is starving fah wuk? Mi wan' to be gran'
Like you Missa D, an' wear pretty clo'es
Like you wife an' you pickney, Lawd doan t'ink a' dose;
An' have mi own bed, an' lovely red rose
Inna mi gyarden, ring 'pan mi finger, bell 'pan mi toes
Like mi learn inna school, me go dey you know
Mi write careful lettah, an' read good, aldough
Mi preffer watch TV or go to a show,
But mi cyan afford dem widouten stay low.

Mi doan wan' mi pickney fallah my paht!
Mi wan' de two gal dem have a nice baht
Like mi see in your room; mi wan' too dat Gyart
Da's mi bwoy, get 'im home an' hyart.

Mi wuk tell mi tyad, mi back fit to break,
Mi have de t'ree pickney, an' belly-ache,
But mi mus' do de night-wuk fi get piece a' cake,
An' smoke up mi spliff to stop mi han' shake.

W'ile you tek up you waters, tell mi fi true
How mi can live an' be happy like you?
Gi' me de anser, gi' mi it, do!
How come for big cash mi have to screw?

A man tell me wance fi go back to de lan',
Fi grow sempaviva* fah cents in mi han'.
Annodda wan tell mi mus' believe in de plan
De Govahment have. *Baas; I do what I can!*

O Gawd, Missa D tell mi de trut'
What mi cyan do wid de res' a' mi yout'?'

Small sweet Jamaican, sweeter than fruit,
My heart bleeds for you; bleeds from its root.

Cirrhosis

(*mod.L., f.Gr.* Kirros *orange-tawney* . . . O.E.D.)

the advance was catlike
stealthy not menacing
an extention of shadow
out of a familiar corner

a blur elongating
easily mistaken
for spreading of the dark
natural and quiet

Semper viva: a herb with medicinal properties now being grown commercially in
Jamaica.

but it moved more swiftly
detaching itself definitely
from the approaching gloom
becoming its own shape and shade

even then not quite distinct
nor demanding strict attention
simply attracting notice
as it approached silently

its catness became eloquent
in that sinuous lope
which is the heritage of panthers
with long consanguineous lineage

of tigers lions leopards
pumas lynxes jaguars
orange-tawny selfish lethal
predators and carnivores

so it was in the flesh
the atavistic shiver
first became manifest
an uneasiness a malaise

unpleasant to acknowledge
impossible to discount
a chilling of the spine
a peristaltic spasm

then the recognition of the creature
the long owned one
nourished and assuaged
by gobbets sops indulgences

but always kept captive
teased for regular amusement
now grown mean and spiteful
ravenous to turn on the tormentor

because it is belonged
it has possession
claims that cannot be ignored
the right to be fed on accustomed meat

it will not be discouraged
its ninth life has its coeval
it is a companion
too gross now to be drowned

Where it's at

Eventually you will find
like others, (no one dropped a name,)
publishers with contracts to be signed,
wine, women, concomitants of fame,
critics polite, sometimes even reverent.
It's turned out somewhat different.

No adoring nubile women
spill champagne: a sofa leaks its straw;
No Abyssinian dulcimers, instead
the solo scratching of the pen
crepitous, an old rat's claw
raking for breakfast and his bed.

Kendel Hippolyte

revo lyric

sweetchile
dem will say dat
dis eh revolution, stop it
dem go talk about
de People an' de Struggle
an' how in dis dry season
t'ings too dread, too serious
for love

as though
love not a serious t'ing
serious like war, frightenin'
tightenin' de heart strings an'
beatin' a rhythm up a twistin' road
all o' we fraid to dance on

love is a serious t'ing
bringin' you back
to baby-helpless trusting nakedness
whether you want or not
if the truth, in real truth
you love

a serious, serious t'ing:
is walking a high high edge
where looking down or back
would end you
yet forward and up
so dark wid no end
love is — a god sweetheart, dey mus' know!
dey can see!

dis instrument we tryin' to make — society
economics — wood and string

den politics — de major key
but de real, real t'ing
de reason an' de melody
de song we want to sing
is love
is love.

come doudou, sing wid me. . .

the air between us (for an expatriate)

the air between us is like glass
when we speak, our words frost

as meanings mist over, i hear you
far off and muffled

I realise that you were shouting
when you walked past you were shouting
your head bent was a scream
that question about coffee was a yell that choked your throat

but you swallowed politely

well, you been swallowing so long
the fire in your belly must be out

for centuries now

that's why the air between us is so cold.

a caribbean exorcism poem

(G.C.)

zombie
is the thing we didn't do
words unsaid and roaming
the life we never lived

bolom
is the hope tormented, unfulfilled
shrivelled to a premature old man
in a baby's body
still-born, still un-born

demon
is dissatisfaction in a mocking shape
the leer of years
contorted grin at ourselves, laughter misused
and coming back at us

and i am the devil
gored by undeeds, prickled restless
by a life that roams inside
despite
a mouth to say it, hands
to shape it

devil, beelzebub, devourer
head-haunter howling in white spaces
serpent, unwanted whisperer
is (if i know it)
the other brother of myself, returning
a difficult counsellor
tortured paradox
eternal parable of our need to love.

Reggae Cat (for Boston Jack)

              Something
in the way these alleys twist and
drop into darkness, how they zag
around a corner, jump a ditch,
rub against a zinc fence as they pass
quiet, quiet, avoiding the street-lamps,
telling you ignore the brightness
trust your feet, you won' fall, listen
to the brotherman ahead of you, he knows
the way, he eh go let you lost —
both of you going the same way, don't it?

              Something
in these alley-shapes, the dark, the scratch
of foot-step   pause   a matchflare
catching the bass bearded voice within
the circle in the yard, within
the sweet smell of smoke saying:
peace and love, me I-dren, peace and love

              Something of all this
stretches inside your sinews till they become guitar strings
trengling under the chop-and-slash
of fingers ratcheting at chords that cry, like
when love hurts you, like
when a lean, lost alley-cat, twisting in her heat
starts wailing:

       skeng-ek
       skeng-ek
       skeng-ek.

Abdur Rahman Slade Hopkinson

Origami

For Tami Fugimoto

A frog, gem-green – like the Jamaican wave –
A paper trinket, hangs from crafty fingers.
Attention, sharpened like a ritual sword,
    Its edge against what's now, what's here,
    Pinpoints your stare.
        You twist and fold
The paper with such wily love –
      It might have been frail leaflets of strange gold.
Your mood's as still as water. The jewel frog
Sings of your passionate exactness.
          Blazing, the sword
    Finds its sweet edge in water's tempering cold.

The Chord

For R.H.

God knows, that's too much terror for your years.
You tell so gamely of the children, dead –
Friends, playmates, neighbours – shot, not on the street,
But indoors, wasted on the cowardly night.
Anthurium lilies of blood, gristle, bone
Bloom on the damp, newspapered walls of home.
A jolly pattern for the children's room.
You do not mention the slack arithmetic
Of undifferentiating machine guns
That, shifting, might have numbered you as well.

The tolling bells alarm
Yet one more on our rope of paradises
Strung at the throat of stunned America.
Predictable, like our tourist-brochure sun,
We see the patterned sequence run
Of old imperial new fraternal war –
History, as repetitious as a gun.

What justice is there for the children – dead?
'None none none none'
Coughs the staccatto gun.

Then label every infant hearse,
Every coffin, with a verse:
A verse, the poet's futile strength and rage.
Link, little poetess, word to singing word.

Each verse excites the Caribbean pattern.
Cued by your grieving, five
Adopted tongues*, five voices cross our sea:
They're scored together in one shuddering chord.

*English, Spanish, French, Dutch, Portuguese – the languages of the Europeans
who colonised Latin America and the Caribbean – now spoken by the native
peoples and those whose ancestors were imported by the Europeans as slaves and
indentured servants. The poem is specifically concerned with tropical Latin
America and the Caribbean.

Arnold H. Itwaru

body rites

(chant eleven)

the fragile light of my fading eyes
lives in the green stillness
of this woodsmoke tremulous moment
a distant fire in this body's night
the nether awakening
beneath the eyelids of another dawn

in the reign of this rain
which dreams us in its fall and flow
even in the venom of each tainted drop
weeping from the skies of our undoing
i gather light
i gather light again and again
and again and again it goes unwilled and unknown
beyond the finity of the pulse
which beats and beats in my blood

above fire and wind i gather
i gather in the heave and flow of our touch
my pleasure my pain
i gather light   i gather   i must
despite the spectral tongues' fanged smiles

again and again i gather
even as my own fragile beating fades
even as i breathe in the green stillness
of our tremulous woodsmoke going
i gather even as it leaves me gathering

and in this carnival

and in this carnival you offer me
the drunkenness of fire
an earful of drums
a dance in my blood –

your face sweats anthems you do not know
your tongue flames the night of my uneasy watch
as you dance you weave you slide past
you return in an applause of bondage
so sweet in our eyes

we have performed
how well have we performed
and now
this stage imprisons us once more

serpent human demon
once more we dance within the barriers of flames,
the audience adores us

we are this carnival are we

Amryl Johnson

Granny in de Market Place

Yuh fish fresh?

Woman, why yuh holdin' meh fish up tuh yuh nose?
De fish fresh. Ah say it fresh. Ah ehn go say it any mo'

Hmmm, well if dis fish fresh den is I who dead an' gone
De ting smell like it take a bath in a lavatory in town
It here so long it happy. Look how de mout' laughin' at we
De eye turn up to heaven like it want tuh know 'e fate
Dey say it does take a good week before dey reach dat state

Yuh mango ripe?

Gran'ma, stop feelin' and squeezin' up meh fruit!
Yuh ehn playin' in no ban'. Meh mango eh no concertina

Ah tell yuh dis mango hard just like yuh face
One bite an' ah sure tuh break both ah meh plate
If yuh cahn tell de difference between green an' rosy red
dohn clim' jus' wait until dey fall down from de tree
Yuh go know dey ripe when de lizard an dem start tuh feed
but dohn bring yuh force-ripe fruit tuh try an' sell in here
it ehn burglars is crooks like all yuh poor people have to fear

De yam good?

Old lady, get yuh nails outta meh yam!
Ah mad tuh make yuh buy it now yuh damage it so bad

Dis yam look like de one dat did come off ah de ark
She brother in de Botanical Gardens up dey by Queens Park
Tourists with dey camera comin' from all over de worl'
takin' pictures dey never hear any yam could be dat ole
Ah have a crutch an' a rocking-chair someone give meh fuh free
If ah did know ah would ah bring dem an' leave dem here fuh she

De bush clean?

Well, I never hear more! Old woman, is watch yuh watching meh
young young dasheen leaf wit' de dew still shinin' on dem!

It seem tuh me like dey does like tuh lie out in de sun
jus' tuh make sure dat dey get dey edges nice an' brown
an' maybe is weight dey liftin' tuh make dem look so tough
Dey wan' build up dey strength fuh when tings start gettin' rough
Is callaloo ah makin' but ah 'fraid tings go get too hot
Yuh bush go want tuh fight an' meh crab go jump outta de pot

How much a poun' yuh fig?

Ah have a big big sign tellin' yuh how much it cos'
Yuh either blin' yuh dotish or yuh jus' cahn read at all

Well, ah wearing meh glasses so ah readin' yuh big big sign
but tuh tell yuh de trut' ah jus' cahn believe meh eye
Ah lookin' ah seein' but no man could be so blasted bol'
Yuh mus' tink dis is Fort Knox yuh sellin' fig as if is gol'
Dey should put all ah all yuh somewhere nice an' safe
If dey ehn close Sing-Sing prison dat go be the bestest place

De orange sweet?

Ma, it eh hah orange in dis market as sweet as ah does sell
It like de sun, it taste like sugar an' it juicy as well

Yuh know, boy, what yuh sayin' have a sorta ring
De las' time ah buy yuh tell meh exactly de same ting
When ah suck ah fin' all ah dem sour as hell
De dentures drop out an' meh two gum start tuh swell
Meh mout' so sore ah cahn even eat ah meal
Yuh sure it ehn lime all yuh wrappin' in orange peel?

De coconut hah water?

Gifts

Is so long she ehn see de man
    man ehn come tuh see she in so long
He was comin' by she every day
    every day every day
bringin' she flowers an presents
    presents an' ting
he in dey wit' she fuh hours
    hours he in dey wit' she
Wen we see she nex' she smilin'
    smilin' like she do somethin' clever
Dat was long pas' look she now
    now look wha' happen tuh she
De man stop callin' so long
    so long he ehn come see she
Look how she belly big
    big like it goin' to buss
An' de girl lookin' so proud
    proud before dey does fall
De girl lookin' in we face an' smilin'
    smilin' like she so somethin' special
Like she feel she do somethin clever
    Clever? any fool can make baby

So ah hah tuh ask she
    she should be hangin' she head in shame
Mavis, wha' de arse yuh hah tuh smile 'bout?
    'bout time she start showin' shame
Miss Ross, yuh too dry up tuh know 'bout love
    Love? Wha' she know 'bout it sheself?
Dis chile is de bes' gift ah could have
    have a bit ah shame ah say
We love child is de bes' gift he could leave
    leave? we KNOW he did leave!
You wouldn't understan' 'bout such tings, Miss Ross
    Miss Ross you shoulda box she mout'
An' de girl stroke she belly an' smile
    smile should be on de other side ah she face
Nuttin' ah tell she could change she mind
    she mind ehn workin' too good
She say she happy as she is
    is love some ah dem does call it, Miss Ross is Love

And Sea

They brought me here to be baptized
among the chicken bones
the tin cans and corroded vomit
to stain the whiteness of my gown
and test the morning of my faith
with the environment of my awareness

Linton Kwesi Johnson

Beacon of Hope

For John La Rose

luminous pyrophorus
in latin letters
cucujos in Mexico?
in english candle fly

the sun fades slowly
behind the distant hill
falls
beyond
today's
horizon
signals the twilight of your dawn

welcome peeni waali fire fly
fine fluorescent gift of night

tonight you will illuminate the path of dreams
like glow-worms of the northern climes
your flashing fluorescence
are eyes of light
flashing sparks
that pierce the dark
of my moonless starless tropical night

welcome nocturnal friend
I name you beacon of hope

tonight fear fades to oblivion
as you guide us beyond the stars
to a new horizon

tomorrow a stranger will enter
my hut my cave my cool cavern of gloom
I will give him bread
he will bring good news from afar
I will give him water
he will bring a gift of light

E. McG. 'Shake' Keane

Soufrière

The thing split Good Friday in two
and that good new morning groaned
and snapped
like breaking an old habit

Within minutes
people
who had always been leaving nowhere
began arriving nowhere
entire lives stuffed in pillow-cases
and used plastic bags
naked children suddenly transformed
into citizens

'Ologists with their guilty little instruments
were already oozing about the mountainsides
bravely
and by radio

(As a prelude to resurrection and brotherly love
you can't beat ructions and eruptions)

Flies ran away from the scene of the crime
and crouched like Pilate
in the secret places of my house
washing their hands

Thirty grains of sulphur
panicked off the phone
when it rang

Mysterious people ordered
other mysterious people
to go to mysterious places
'immediately'

I wondered about the old woman
who had walked back to hell
to wash her Sunday clothes

All the grey-long day
music
credible and incredibly beautiful
came over the radio
while the mountain refreshed itself

Someone who lives
inside a microphone
kept things in order

Three children
in unspectacular rags
a single bowl of grey dust between them
tried to manure the future
round a young plum tree

The island put a white mask
over its face
coughed cool as history
and fell in love with itself

A bus travelling heavy
cramped as Calvary
thrust its panic into the side of a hovel
and then the evening's blanket
sent like some strange gift from abroad
was rent by lightning

After a dream
of rancid hope and Guyana rice
I awoke to hear
that the nation had given itself
two hundred thousand dollars

The leaves did not glisten when wet

An old friend
phoned from Ireland
to ask about the future
my Empire cigarettes
have lately been tasting of sulphur
I told her that.

Week Seven

JAZZ, the Sane Man said,
is a bit like surgery. You need it.
You buy it privately, or you socialise it
if you dare.
Also, it purifies by probing – even in public.
Cuts out the stuff and nonsense. But
it tends to heal sweeter if the instruments
are not too sterilised.

Paul Keens-Douglas

Trinidad if ah let yu

Trinidad if ah let yu
Yu would make me angry
Trinidad if ah let yu
Yu would make me cry
Trinidad if ah let yu
Yu would make me fly
Away to foreign climes
An' maybe worse
Or better times.
Trinidad if ah let yu
Yu would make me feel
Dat yu don't really care
Trinidad if ah let yu
Yu would kill me wit' despair
Trinidad if yu let me
Ah could love yu.

Wukhand

Sah gimme ah wuk nah.
An lookin ole but ah strong.
Never mind ah skinny sah,
Ah could wuk like ah beas.
Ask anybody, ask dem sah:
Clean yard, shine car, cut grass,
Ah tekkin anyting sah.
Yu see dis hand sah, it like stone
Never mind it lookin marga.
Dis hand could pelt cutlass

Like Sampson pelt de ass jaw,
Dis hand clear bush from Toco to Town,
When tree see me dey does bawl;
If dey could ah run, is ah straight case,
Cause I is de man with de Lightnin in me hand.
Me blade does flash in de sun
Like fish gainst river stone,
An when ah finish, is me one standin
An all bush lay down, quiet quiet.
Yes sah, dis hand is a wukkin hand.
Yu lookin at me sah,
With me pants foot roll up,
An me mareno lookin holy, holy,
Never mind dat sah; look sah, look me hand
Tough like mangrove root,
Hard like iron cable.
Dis is ah hand sah, ah real hand, ah wukkin hand,
Ah hand with ah past, ah present an ah future.
Dis hand chuck banana, sah,
Cut dem, draw dem, an stack dem,
Under sun, under moon, an in de dark,
An when de back cry out, an foot say stop,
Dis hand still goin like ah champ,
Ah stroke to de left, an ah stroke to de right.

Dat was me, de man with de iron hand.
Dont judge me by me size sah,
Ah lookin' small, ah know dat,
But me hand sah, watch it.
Dis hand have character,
Dis hand throw net like was feather,
An when dis hand pull back sah,
Was fish in any weather.
Ah catch dem, cut dem, clean dem
Ah couldn't afford to eat dem.
Yes sah, dis is ah hand sah.

When dis hand was ah boy sah,
It throw stone, pelt rock,
Wash in river, an cook on fire.
It get cut, bruise, bounce, burn, an break.
Dis hand sah, grow up strong.
It help police pull hose
When man house start burnin down,
It tired pullin car out ah ditch,
It break fight under plenty strain,
But is ah wukkin hand sah.
An dis hand sah, have touch,
Crack ah egg, pick ah flower,
Caress ah woman, ahhhh, sah
As gentle as de mornin sun
Growin fierce, but not destroyin
Beautiful sah, beautiful.
An dis hand have speed sah,
Yes speed.
See dis hand sah, pull ace sah,
From any part ah de pack,
An so it pullin ace, is so it wukkin hard.
But dis hand is ah honest hand sah.
Dis hand pick up two hundred dolla
Lying dey in open street,
An dis hand send it straight to de station.
Yes sah, dis hand make headline,
De paper call me de 'honest hand'.
Wha yu say sah?
Yu eh have no wuk?
Yu making joke sah.
How yu mean yu eh have wuk?
Ah rick lookin fella like yu,
Stand up in front yu big house,
An dress up as if is weddin yu going to.
Ah know is joke yu jokin sah,
But dis hand could take ah joke.

What sah? dis is not yu house?
Yu just stan up here waitin on taxi?
But look me crosses with dis niggerman,
Ah stan up here only wastin me time with he,
Ah poor man like me, with arthritis,
Me dam hand near fallin off,
An he can't even sponsor ah cup ah coffee.
Only posing up in front de people place.
Ah have a good mind to arrest yu.
Look man, move out ah me sight yu hear?
Before ah leggo de hand on yu.
Well, yes.

Anthony Kellman

Bajan

. . . and now I see you once
again and drench my body with your brown sand,
squatting here on the limpid beach over which pelicans,
out to search their living in the sea, glide
softly as spears.
You are the sea, a child impatient with your castle
that melts like some dethroned waxen god,
while your image keeps wringing and wringing the heart.
I come back again, the Bajan castaway tumbling
across those rakish seas.

Worlds overlap
whirl in arcs of islands
There is only the grey mass of twilight
and nothing's fixed in one place
The peaceful face squats
on a turbulent heart
and the moon in the sun

Where does one begin?
from the cliff's edge? or from the bottom
of the hill which isn't a hill?
(See! Your back moans halfway up the flat incline!)
I end up where I start
(on every bone and muscle of this land)
where all is well and unwell

and then the cry of sunrise
and the conch shell.

The King

An old man with fire in his eyes.
A steep hill. A love song.
Man, how far have you come?

Another year has passed,
Posterity clutches another page,
But the only one to have come of age
is the old man, fire leaping in his eyes.

Halfway up the sharp incline
and my old man is moving still.
Sweating? yes. Groaning? yes.
But climbing climbing still.

Friends of mine I've grown up with have withered
in one short year. Jacki's fifth child crawls
over her shrivelled 20 year-old breasts. No joke!
George got electric shock
for 'smoking too much herb'.
In gardens framed with inverted coke
bottles or four-foot high guard walls –
bleached sunflowers, sometimes a dead bird.

Looka! The wrinkled old man is still smiling,
climbing; he still bearing he cross, hear!
Looka! His flaming eyes still rivet the sun;
nothing's lost, nothing's lost, hear!

New frocks and fresh faces burst
like Christmas morning,
Shoes creak their newness for the 5 o'clock service,
The day wrestles with the diminishing darkness.
A steep hill. Another year.
An old man singing:
'Some folks are goin' to see their king'.

Jane King

Clichés for an Unfaithful Husband

So. The game was worth the candle.
Was the candle worth the cake?
Now you have it and you eat it
Does it make your belly ache?

Hymn

For you I would put on embroidered robes
I would henna the palms of my hands
and the soles of my feet.
I would ornament myself with gold
drape myself in gilt and scarlet
stroke silver bronze mandalas round my eyes.
I oil my breasts
I perfume my body
my hair is washed and scented
my body cleansed.
Already the mounting rhythm's heartbeat drumthrob
Prepares a way for you.
With prayer and preparation
and mystic decoration
I would dance for you
I would sing for you
I would be your priestess, your handmaiden.

I would be a channel for your throbbing magic
your thrusting power, glistening
jewelled, and beyond singing beautiful:
mosque-domed spear of shining bronze
marble-hard, silk-smooth, warm as flesh
I would adore with all my hands
would slide its warrior length
encircling its strength's dense circumference
I would feel your power's gliding slick
warm hard beat deep deep deep
within me, through me, open me, fill me
feel it, feel it, feel it, feel THAT –
life force of universe welling to gush here
swelling to rush where
no mind is needed to know
(if mind could be heeded now)
what is love.
As above
so below.
I would be the channel for our creating
flesh magic fecund recreating
reaching All –
I would be your priestess, your handmaiden.

Moments:

Always it's moments glimpsed while journeying past.
A darkened hill beneath pale yellow sky.
A shivering sense of peace. It does not last.

Soft smoke drifts slowly, seen through glass
and misty sheets of silvering rain pass by.
Always it's moments glimpsed while journeying past.

A jostling market crowd – colours, shrill, fast –
vision evaporates without a sigh.
A shivering sense of peace. It does not last.

A pale sun hangs above a blackened mast
a horror that the self itself will die.
Always it's moments glimpsed while journeying past.

An orange sun and pools of silvered purple cast
on glistening asphalt. A sense of one – not-I.
A shivering sense of peace. It does not last.

A sense of home, of peace. Driving too fast
seeking to lose a sense of sinking by...
Always it's moments glimpsed while journeying past.
A shivering sense of peace. It will not last.

John Robert Lee

Lusca

For Derek Walcott

> . . .*in you, the forever lost has berthed*
> *the might-have-been is beached*
> *and glimpses anchored*. . .

Caught in my private limbo, my
youth lost in a ravine somewhere
between town and suburb,
I never knew anyone like you,
my Lusca.

Moonlit rings I never knew,
their songs, or dances, chances for first gropings in the dark;
never had I known, like you, grandmothers and their days of
    pride,
chantwelles for this feast-day or that. . .

Dropping behind the crossed bars
of my parents' pride and poverty,
I sailed alone to meet my heroes
on Europe's passages of glory.

And you, your early gods were rum-soaked banjo-players,
wanderers of hills and towns, story-tellers, gossip-mongers,
to whom you gave your heart up captive, new each time, to each
    new chord,
to each sweet tongue of flute that whistled you past long canoes,
down lonely tracks, to rivers hiding naked among rocks
and frowning rain forests.

While wolves and wicked wizards held
me rigid and afraid to move
on nights when hell itself had seemed
to choose our roof for lechery
unimagined,
you knew, my little Lusca, of old crones dégagéd;
of strange and silent single men who, they said, might have
    mounted you,
you dear Lusca, in their magec noire! You knew as I did not
of soucouyants and loup-garous, of kélé and kutumba,
of chembois and of obeah!

Books could make me fear the dark, but your grandmother,
head scarved, nostrils flaring, could flame her mist-ringed eyes
    and send you
quick to bed or straight to father-priest's confessional:

> — duh lajablesse is coming!
>> — M'sieu Luwoi et Papa Bois!
>>> — Look! duh screaming faceless Bolom
>>> searching for Ti-Jean and Lusca!

Aieee!

>>>> — poor jab, poor Lusca.

And so dear Lusca I have a loss to claim:
my friends must know that town bred as I am,
my hands are soft, my feet cling poorly to the land;
my fingers scratch in vain, my toes itch for shoes to wear;
here, I am Lusca's lover, nice boy, but still from town;
the earth will not be entered by my hoe, it cannot conceive
that I can truly want its syllables of roots, its language of
firm green shoots that climb from it with confidence and with
    trust.

A stranger here, my seeds grow weak-kneed, if they grow, and
   lack truth;
no one believes them, their garbled language making them the
   village idiots.

And this is why dear Lusca I must remain a lover
and have but safe acquaintance with your past;
or every image in your dusty album
will fill me with a morbid lust
when each deserves my gratitude.

  My plot of ground is dry and hard
as sidewalks are; at nights street lamps
block out the stars and hi-fi sets
replace the country violons;
and I must dig foundations deep,
plunge steel and concrete shafts into
this city's dirt, and hope for structures firm,
and spare, no space for flair or show,
each entrance, passage, exit, clear and marked,
each section storing much within a little space.

  Perhaps dear Lusca we should build our house
somewhere on a valley's side, a valley moving
with its riverbed, between the country and the town;
then we would see the city's lights
and hear the dying belle-aire drums;
comb the dust of highways off our hair
and smell the burners' blue-smoked pits.
Perhaps.

Vocation

For Patrick Anthony, priest and folklorist

And so, despite the whisperings
behind hands clasped in fervent unbelief,
despite the stale, old lady's scent
of righteousness that crawls from
$\qquad\qquad\qquad$ under French soutanes;
despite all that, and more

this is yours, you, your claim on love.

They could have asked. They could have asked
the blue-smoked hills, the country mandolins,
old trembling-nosed, broad-voiced chantwelles
they could have asked; they could have asked tracks lost
but for some village's dying song;
$\qquad$ and belle-aire drums
$\qquad$ and violons
$\qquad$ and moonlit ragged choirs,
$\qquad$ could have told and would have told
of what they'd always known:
that like a hidden mountain stream
caught patient swirling past the ages of the land
nothing dims that vision waiting gently:
$\qquad$ of calm clean pools below the waterfall.

And I
who share a common celibacy
that priests and poets must endure,
search the purity of syllable
seeking truths you've found;
incensed with love, I make too
that ritual of Word and Gesture,
wrists uplifted, fingers plucking
outward, scratching at this altar,
daring faith and hope, changing them
into some clarity.

Mango

On Sunday afternoons in mango season,
Alleyne would fill his enamel basin
with golden-yellow fruit, wash them in clean water,
then sit out in the yard, under the grapefruit tree,
near the single rose bush, back to the crotons,
place the basin between his feet,
and slowly eat his mangoes, one by one, down to the clean white
    seed.
His felt-hat was always on his head. The yellow basin, chipped
    near the bottom,
with its thin green rim, the clear water, the golden fruit,
him eating slowly, carefully, picking the mango fiber from his
    teeth,
under those clear, quiet afternoons, I remember.
Me sitting in the doorway of my room, one foot on the steps that
    dropped
into the yard, reading him, over a book. That's how it was.

E. A. Markham

Don't Talk to Me about Bread

she kneads
deep into the night
and the whey-coloured dough

springy and easy and yielding to her will

is revenge. Like a rival,
dough toys with her. Black-brown hands in the belly
bringing forth a sigh.

She slaps it, slaps it double with fists
with heel of hand applies the punishment
not meant for bread

and the bitch on the table sighs
and exhales a little spray of flour
a satisfied breath of white

on her hand

mocking the colour
robbing hands of their power
as they go through the motions, kneading. . .
She listens for the sigh which haunts

from the wrong side of her own door
from this wanton cheat of dough
this whey-faced bitch rising up

in spite of her fight, rising up
her nipples, her belly, rising up
two legs, dear god, in a blackwoman's rage. . .

Laughing at her, all laughing at her:
giggling bitch, abandoned house, and Man
still promising from afar what men promise. . .

Hands come to life again: knife
in the hand, the belly ripped open, and she smears

white lard and butter, she sprinkles
a little obeah of flour and curses to stop up the wound.

Then she doubles the bitch up
with cuffs, wrings her like washing
till she's the wrong shape

and the tramp lets out a damp, little sigh
a little hiss of white
enjoying it.

Herstory

My name is easy to pronounce, isn't it?
— reward for being young and gliding
towards the heart of the world. History
of a family helped us to travel with travelling
as an option. Though we hoped, by luck,
to arrive somewhere. And after these thirty years'
sojourn, no one will say if this has happened.

Sons seemed designed to ease the travel:
we were young, could produce our own army,
could translate dreams into marks in the dust (a flight
of fancy which warmed some who shuddered in the ship,
   panicked in aircraft).

They say it would take time: we were prepared
better than ancestors. I forget
if they were right. Now, children have grey hairs
and rest between journeys.

And here I am, half by choice, visited
by family. I am at home, they say: others
with difficult names manage exile. My speech
is recognizable; grown men with casualness
of boys call me mother. They do it
eating grapes at my table; without comment working out
riddles at the foot of the bed.

And from time to time something stirs
in them, like the days before they were here
when we trickled in from the edge,
from the foot of a body whose face
was still in the clouds, with words primed to conquer
territory hard as this. . .
Now they come to avenge violence
done to a stranger – that far woman
separated from family; this man – this TV face –
exiled in his own country, hospitalized,
yet young enough to be photographed, for love
to have the old meanings. . .
Their freedom is what these children
half-strive for. They are skilled in grand
impossible names, not like mine.
Too late for me to dissent. But children
have children: there's comfort in that.

Marc Matthews

Realarro

I love the
friday night
smell of
mammie baking
bread — creeping
up to me in
bed
& tho I fall
asleep before I
even get a bite
I know for sure
when
morning come
the kitchen table
will be laden
with bread
fresh & warm.
salt bread
sweet bread, crisp
& brown &
best of all
coconut buns
make me
love the friday
night smell of
mammie baking bread
putting me to bed
to sleep
dreaming

Come Come

lea we go pun
D-seawall
Bus D-bottle
Sing D-song
pitch we XM melody
against D-sea
watchin the overboards
wit – dem short-time
Cast-net ketchin'
Respectable
Bigfish
No rent fuh pay
Seawall like backseat
always free.
Come lea we go
pun D-seawall
talk ole time story
debate questions
political with
plantation philosophy
watch Dem picknee
like crab march
dance an play
duck an drake in
d-sea

Come lea we go
pun d-seawall
Cut d-baby hair
tek it – mek sacrifice
to mumma sea
gather fuh make puja
puja
throw the flowers
garland d-sea
Come-Baptize
Duck the New Born
Come Read the word
Sister
fire nex time roun'
Come buil the
pyre
pour D-ghee
Light D-fire
Scatter D-ashes
inna D-sea

Come Come
Lea we go
pun D-seawall
See if Fairmaid
Leff she comb
fah we.

Marina Ama Omowale Maxwell

Our Revolutions Must Be Different

For Mikey Smith, Dobru and Maurice Bishop

Warrior/Houngan we salute you
Frail body
Towering Spirit
It is a savagery/that you have known.

Our Revolutions *must* be different.

Limping wizard
Prophet of the tribe
It is a brutality/visited upon you.

Our Revolutions *must* be different.

'It is not
It is not
It is not enough' –
to make a change
To make blood
To make slaughter

Our Revolutions *must* be different

Our poets cannot be eaten
Our shepherds cannot be stoned
We rip out the logos of our beginnings
We trample the heaven-heart of our growth

Our Revolutions *must* be different.

Somehow we must shape warrior
with houngan
Bury between us the antelope's humerus
The Austrolapithecus horn
Somehow we must claim amazon
with mambo.

Rise beyond scalpel and missile
Reach up for quantum and love

Our Revolutions *must* be different
Reshaping landscapes of hope
Remembering our beginnings
After blood must come pansong
and wing

Rhythmic tremors/Rockers brothers
It is a savagery, a brutality, a slaughter —
But your voice is our song
And will reggeh down the drum-tracks of time.

WARRIOR/HOUNGANS WE SALUTE YOU

I Expect an Orchid

Sometimes today
I am an old tree
discolouring
growing fungus
spreading slowly on my bark
a pink filigree, reaching slowly –
I cast no seeds.

But
I expect an orchid
to grow out of the pool
of one eye, though
Aged hanas coil around my neck
blocking my forests
Grow long in tendons
in my arms, and legs
and one day, slowly, slowly
will root me
subsiding silently
to the earth

Till then, I dance, slowly, slowly
turning, still turning
from my grave
of space
still hoping, again
every hoping, once more
to fly . . .
Since
I expect an orchid, any day, now . . .

Ian McDonald

The Place they have to go

When someone checks into Mercy Ward
One of the particulars you have to get
Is what provision has been made
For a burial costing nothing, net.
They look restless and turn away.
Even if you have a few days only
You don't want to think of the black hearse
Pulled by the half-blind City horses
Or about Merriman's fourth best limousine
Rattling unattended through the streets.
And you don't want to know
About that part of the graveyard
Where no flowers grow, just tussocky grass
And nettles and black-ant nests.

You often have to visit where they go:
A bare field where goats are grazed,
Rust-coloured grasshoppers whirring as you step.
Across the way the splendid tombs arise
White and shaded by huge impressive trees:
Marble blossoms deck them down the years.
And ornaments and wreaths in perfect alabaster.
But here of course no monuments arise:
Graves dug in line straight into earth.
When freshly dug slap-dash dirt-mounds show
With wooden crosses stuck awry on top:
Rain crumbles them shapeless in a month or so.
This field of grass and goat-weed
Holds a bare and hopeless dignity.

The Supervisor's office is a simple place:
A chair, a desk, a concrete vault
Where archives of all burials are kept;
The leather-covered volumes stretch centuries back.
It sets things in perspective right away:
The record is equal in these careful books,
Inscribes for all an austere common fate.
No space for high or space for low:
The line of written detail does not change,
All are put down here the same,
Bare, unblemished soul-mates, row on row.
In the field you do not get to see
The part of burial that does not show
Obscurity or utmost fame:
The scene below is much the same.

The Poison-maker

I

Travelled miles that day
Gold savanna sun to shadows of darkest green.
A day of such beauty
I have not seen before,
The air gleaming like the start of the world.
On the edge of forest
Hawks hanging in the blue heaven:
Black wings beat once
And they are aloft forever.

They have always been in this great sky
Eyes scanning the long horizons
Where suns have burnt to black the short-grass valley-fields
Amidst orchid-covered granite blocks of white
Gold and scarlet cocks-of-the-rock sport and fight.
Then the dense-dark forest green:
In the cold creek canopied with branches
The bright, dark-red water runs like wine.
Mora-trees, breaking into new leaf everywhere,
White, liver-coloured, green, and deepest red
Stand like huge chandeliers in ancient rooms.

II

Flashing messengers of light and swiftness,
Grey-blue kingfishers lead downstream to a village.
Well-kept habitations in a green glade:
Bustle with life, women bake and cut,
Children play with rolling balls of silverballi wood.
Hunting dogs snooze amidst the cooking smoke.
Red-stained hammocks swing in evening air,
Strings of red beads are heaped for market day
Making mounds of brilliance on the brown earth floor.

*   *   *

Relaxed, at ease, on mats of yellow cloth,
Chewing Indian corn parched white as jasmine buds,
The men extend an unsuspicious welcome,
Offer pepper-hot iguana eggs and wild red cherries,
Cool, week-old paiwari spiced with sugar-gum.
Their eyes are black and impenetrably bright.
It looks a place well-settled in good routines.

*   *   *

Alone, outside the evening light,
Alone with black arrows,
Who is that man, wrapped in black,
Squatting in twin-circles of dropped black pods,
Crouched like a crow, stirring a black pot
Sizzling on red embers like a black cat spitting?
A chant of mourning comes from this figure of the night.
Why does no one approach him? Why so far removed?
Why will he never join the hum of life and light?
They shrug and smile like children who are happy:
'The poison-maker,' they murmur, 'he is the poison-maker.'

Life/Death

Sudden,
Quick as light:
Skin shine,
Then
Bone white.

Anthony McNeill

Straight Seeking

Many believe one day the ship
will drop anchor at Freeport,
but now it's enough to praise
high on the s'liff. The smoke-
blackened city wounds instant
divines to enter their pipes
like dreams. Tonight Jah
rears in a hundred tenements
missed by my maps.
Still compassed by reason,
my ship sails cooly between
Africa and heaven.

Hello Ungod

ungod my lungs blacken
the cities have fallen
the easy prescriptions
have drilled final holes in my cells
ungod my head sieves in the wind
ungod I am sterile
ungod it appears
I am dying
ungod I am scared
ungod can you hear me
ungod I am testing for levels
ungod testing 1 2 3
ungod are you evil
ungod I can't hear you

ungod I am trying
ungod I can't reach you
ungod my lungs blacken
the cities have fallen
head sieves in the wind

ungod disconnecting

*   *   *

write through the night
the woman is glass

her voice is in fragments
so rough to the touch

we are swimming
I say to her come

follow me   I say
I am water and light

I am air
I take the last road

the woman is water
inside me

the name wakes the first voice
it says you are nothing

you drowned a long time
then the blue like a great bell

rang in the clearing
the presences ring

you drowned a long time
follow me

me fire you fish
we will wake each other

rain falling
the planets

have blessed me each day
the nightingale sang it

no name

*   *   *

Olive
hang like a bell

stay
I love you

the long day with its lights
if I ever come out

if I do
if I ever come

live with me
love me

lady of sea

Mark McWatt

A Man in the House

She wonders
why I'm still here
so long after the wedding cake,
after the beach house,
after the hand-in-hand shopping
for all those things that purr in the kitchen
like cats.

She seems curious
that there's always this face
in a corner of her full-length mirror,
this form that spaniels her
from room to fresh-swept room,
this voice that's always asking questions
instead of favours.

'Who *are* you, really?'
The question flutters behind her eyes
but has never got past those firm lips;
so we still brush against each other in bed
and collide in front the fridge.
She knows I have not cried
recently, that I probably pay the rent;

and now she begins to suspect me
of loitering
with intent. . .

The Boat Builder

Ignatio lived on the river
with his wife and little daughter

he built the boats that ran the river
he and his wife built their daughter

Ignatio never slept at night
his plans of perfection multiplied

in the silence of his factory
the builder fidgeted sleeplessly

the wake of his genius splintered the moon
in the river's fragments he heard a groan

Immaculata (his only daughter)
woke that night and turned to stone.

Marcellino, the new boat builder,
is a happy, wealthy man

with his wife and little son
he sleeps while night-horses run

Ignatio still lives on the river
on a granite outcrop, all alone.

Lady Northcote

And she must have looked
like a governor's lady
when they flung champagne at her
long time ago; all polished wood
and brass and delicate white
for the tropics.

But when I first saw her
at the stelling at Kumaka
– a raw teenager out for kicks –
she seemed excitingly abused,
had taken her licks
from years of men and sea
with her pride and style intact
– or just sufficiently drained
that she could notice the attentions
of a mere boy like me.

When the storm hit
four hours out from Waini Point
she danced as in a fit,
nostalgic for her frolic of the past
when she sparkled with polished brass
and with the wit of those
who journeyed for the fun of it.
She plunged and reared,
taking the breaking wave upon her breast
– flat and hard now, and dun,
but comforting, none the less,
especially to a traveller like me,
still young enough to think
that strong women are the best.

Then, in the grey light before dawn,
she slipped quietly into harbour:
breathless, mysterious, a little naughty
– like all the 'perfect ladies'
of my adolescent dreams.

Stone

He found a fossil
on the underside of a stone.
He wondered how many million years ago
the creature lived outside the stone.
He was filled with wonder,
all alone,
on the empty beach where he found it;
but then he turned and looked
at the hard sky.

Pauline Melville

Honor Maria

Honor Maria, I see you
Sitting at your typewriter
Surrounded by wild fig trees
Bound with dark green Elephants' Ears
Dry rustling Mother-in-law's tongue
Whispers ceaselessly by the stone trellis
As you tap-tap out the tale
Of Hilda Riot's battle with Mawga lion –
To which Mrs Orange-Hat bore silent witness –
Or tap-tap out the sagas of street-vendors
Who fly, upright, through the air from Haiti
With boxes of raisins under their arms.
A dark mother, familiar with the names of plants
Birthed a daughter
Eyes green as Negril sea,
Hair blonde as the golden sea-horse
That dances upside down in the waves.
Fair Jamaica.

Honor Maria, I see you
Where the wild cane grows
Near the river at Castleton,
Or standing on that rackety bridge
By the deserted sugar mill.
But, I daresay,
You are, right now, in downtown Kingston
Up to your ankles in the garbage
That steams through gutters
After torrential rain,
Railing, with silver-bangled fist,
At the murder of your friends,
And cursing because the car won't start.

Bruised by Jamaican stones,
Deserted by Mafu
(for a Japanese reggae band)
Serenaded by seventy revolutionaries
From a neighbouring island,
You still made in tree tops
A sanctuary for the strange women artists
Of your own country.
Honor Maria, I see you
Hacking poetry from the undergrowth
Of Cockpit Country,
Pummelling plays from the shanty-town,
Snatching at the last bottle of sweet white wine
From the supermarket shelf,
Reclining, in Violet's freshly laundered skirt,
On the patchwork bedspread,
Stabbing at the paper with your angry pen.
And all the while, Stonyhill dogs bark
At phantom gunmen under the banyan tree.

Stonebridge Park Estate

Hyacinth is not yet used
To living in the sky.
She sits, jangling gold bangles,
Chains and anklets,
On the magic red patterned carpet,
T.V. in the corner,
Eating figs.

A cold wind howls through
The derelict haunted walkways in space.
The lift with steel doors
Hums upwards towards the North Star.

Hyacinth sits in state
In her small room in the sky,
Hair braided and beaded,
Elbow on the carved leather footstool from home,
Hand upon her jaw,
Watching 'Dynasty'.

A piece of El Dorado in Harlesden.

Homeland

The old colonial house,
My father's birthplace,
White shuttered, wooden slatted,
Sags and settles on its haunches.
A lewd stripteaze of peeling paint
Reveals grey, sun-bleached timbers,
Exposing the house for what it is –
A brothel.

Relentlessly indifferent,
The sun hangs, a metallic sphere in space,
Over the small town of New Amsterdam.

History too, it seems,
Tired of the sandflies,
Has packed its bags and emigrated
From this land of many waters
Somewhere behind God's back.

I am standing
On the dark, varnished wooden floor,
Mosquito nets – obscene bridal veils
Hang in the breezeless air.
My father, as a child,
Leans from the window,
Gazing out,
Eyes deep with unfathomable histories,
At the armies of clouds that march
Across the wide, wide skies from Venezuela,
Destined for other horizons.
Eventually, he was to follow them.

Darkness falls.
Together we listen to the tree-frogs
Outside the house
Which perches so precariously
On the edge of this vast continent
Of perpetual decay.
And a voice wails out
From the ancient juke-box in the bottom-house:
'Take me by the hand
And lead me to the land
Of ecstasy.'

Ras Michael

Preface

I stood watching
the parade of floats
and masqueraders
hiding my culture in a
pair of rubber slippers
and feeling like Cuffy with-
out a revolution
when a daughter
anxious of her colour pointed a finger
of european manufacture
and said,
'Aren't you anti-government?'
i said
'you must be mistaken;
my locks are long because
i can't afford a razor-blade
and i have no friends
in ROME'
Then everybody turns around
and starts handing me golden arrow-
heads
whilst over at the culture centre
Pandit Ramfoot
in african lion-cloth and
amerindian blow-pipe
reads poetry to the non-aligned
nations.
As imitate on this
the daughter of european manufacture
becomes commercial

and rapes my ego by severing
herself
from my umbilical cord
which, by now
is as hard as modern mathematics
'i have accepted revolution,
but it has not accepted me,' i tell her
and immediately she
turns into a dollar bill
with the picture of an american
actor wearing a hammer and a sickle.
i sigh,
and stoop down on to the
concrete pavement
to re-write history
when a sexy looking post girl brings
an official telegram
informing me that the masses now have
leaders
and that all poets must attend
a competition to plan
another revolution
i immediately get up and
buy a pair of rubber-slippers
a passport
a bob marley l.p.
and a air-line ticket to south africa.

Rooplall Monar

Koker

I

Belly waves roll upon waves
climbing on top the other
as unfulfilled lovers do
tumbling in whirlpools
at the end of desire,
then come splashing me in the face
drunk with the power of temporal grace.

But who knows
who ever knows the beginning of this dual agony?

I still wonder why the endurance
of sun-cracked weather,
silent carrion-crow clouds
white unending unending distance

Sometimes I question the origin of my birth
and the riddle of the proverbs:
who first saw the maker of this life,
or heard the first cry of creation?

I bear like pregnant paddy sheaves
everlasting burden of three months' rain
savannah surging waters.

They come, lost little children
seeking my age-old counsel.

I turn to myself and ponder
'Perhaps I am life-and-death –
yet I am neither
for unseeming tapestries weave
and weave. . .'

Out there in the ocean
something silently speaks with me
and only the wink of my eyes understand:
Am I sun or rain?
Am I godmother
to crabs, shrubs, courida?

Still they come
children of a lost land
into crevices of my worn-out body,
listening to that age-old dirge
afraid of the flood

Another worthless death –
for what?

I long to have the Atlantic winds
turn my wings
begin again the patterns of my life.
I hunger for the voices of the oceans,
fishing boats by my pillars
stars of the night.

But do I serve
Man or Gods?

For I am neither life nor death,
drowned in age and ceremonies,
eyes for ever in question:
symbols
estrangement
seasons

On this curved punt bridge
I watch wrinkled black waters
sail away into eyeless savannahs
where sleep embryonic chinks
of a rebirth

This lonely watch-house by the bridge
reminds me of past love,
undying midday caresses –
my soul breaks into ripples
like a lump of dry earth
falling in a cool clear creek.

Sometimes my stunted bones crack
like burning bamboo joints
in the hot scorpion sun
as I remember the ordeal of
a twin baptism,
a twin consciousness

In dew-wet mornings
when crouching baboons listen half-asleep
and streaks of rain-smoke
settle on edges of limp canes,

I feel an unutterable joy,
a desire to clasp this horizon in my palms
becoming God and Man of these fields,
but past footprints,
shadows of a barbarous ritual,
follow me like an epileptic fit
whenever the first mule-whip crack,
breaks the morning silence

In distant clouds
tales turn within the seasons
and sprinkling drops of rain
bless the sacrifice
when carrion crows are crowned
at ceremonies of another death-in-birth

I die many times in my sleep
in the mornings
I am old, old and strange
with a mind-telling agony
without origins
yet deep and meaningful

Yet how many times I totter
clutching impotent gods?
Succumb to these brutish
umbilical cords?
Among ruins and copper trunks
a voice forever wails
with the rushing winds.

II

Tides of rain and thunder
carved lines on my forehead,
my hard-corned palms
keep secrets of the soil
and courses of the winds.
Yet I am unable to decipher parables
of myself.

Here fields, savannahs, paddy sheaves
and the profile of myself
in the reflection of the stream:
A new day! a new day!
Signs of the marriage of many horizons
in these fields.

Judgement Day

Plants shrivelled
earth parched
rats and roachs
inhabit the water pipe
so long it has been dry

In the socket of the eye
is an emptiness.
Is this our judgement day?

Pamela Mordecai

Easy Life

So you haven't had a very
easy life. Well, you must tell me
which way you walk that you didn't choose.
which one you lie with that you didn't
fancy; which dirt you eat but you
never scrape it together eagerly.
yea, greedily, with your own
hands. . .

            Who can have
a clear ear for your plight? The red ones,
crazy with the sun, howling
their misconstructions at the sky?
Children dragging bellies heavy
with their fathers' seed to monstrous
beginnings? Who born twist? Who
born dead? Who chop before they born?
I not even dealing with hungry:
hungry is them same
greedy hands, scratching up dirt:
not dealing with sick neither:
sick is the wriggling things that
turn up when dirt scratch.

I am saying, did someone teach
you to name things? Chew food so you
could swallow? Hide you behind
a door and offer to evil men
her breasts for their distraction?

Say to you, 'No, you can have some,
but pickney, never everything'? Say
to you, 'No mind, whatever, it will
pass'? Whisper, almost at the end
'Ecstasy also, that too, that will pass'?
Say to you, 'Everyday
give thanks, give praise'?

She prayed who set her back
against the world to plant
you deep for long life
and everyday gave thanks.

Last Lines

This is the last line I draw.
Alright. Draw the last line.
But I tell you, yonder
is a next. No line ever last,
no death not forever.
You see this place? You see it?
All of it? Watch it good.
Not a jot nor a tittle
going lost. Every old
twist-up man you see,
every hang-breast woman,
every bang-belly pickney,
every young warrior
who head wrench
with weed, white powder,
black powder, or indeed
the very vile persuasion
of the devil – for him not
bedridden you know –

every small gal-turn-woman
that you crucify on the
cross of your sex
before her little naseberry
start sweeten,
I swear to you,
every last one shall live.
Draw therefore, O governor,
prime minister, parson,
teacher, shopkeeper,
politician, lecturer,
resonant revolutionaries,
draw carefully
that last fine line
of your responsibility.

Starapple Tree

The wind
turns back

its leaves
I see

their
undersides

and know
always

the other
faces.

Mervyn Morris

Pre-Carnival Party

(after a poem by Jules Romain)

One evening in another town
— a little before Carnival —
a funny man with flies around
him crashed into a bar

'Beauty-queen an' sagaboy,' he said,
'dey posin', but dey ain' fool me:
de one sure t'ing is all-yuh dead
did time nex' century:

'yuh lookin' vague an' sad like when
yuh ain' know what to-duh.
Look alive! Before ah sen'
de side fo' yuh!'

Reminded of the loyal flies
buzzing round his face,
the people quickened into life —
jumped up and shook the place.

On what it was that made us jump,
injecting life into the fete,
the pundits waver or are dumb.
Was it the fear of flies or death?

Pilate

And then I tried to pass the buck;
but Herod, with astute aplomb,
politely, sent him back.

I tried to move the people
to accept he might be freed
this feast of The Passover.
'Kill him! Kill him! Nail him
to the cross!' They clamoured for
Barabbas, insurrectionist, a bandit
who's attacked imperial rule.
'Try Jesus for yourselves,' I told the mob;
'You judge him by your law.'
'Kill him,' they hollered louder,
'Nail him to the cross!'
Then slimy priests, those holy rogues
of politics, began to turn the screws:
'You must not fail to sentence Christ,
soi-disant King of Jews.
Your masters wouldn't like it much
if we should let them know
we caught a man supplanting Rome
and you have let him go.'

My basic job is keeping peace
and reverence for Rome. The man
was bad for both. I had to yield.
'I find no fault in him,' I cried,
and ordered water brought;
and, public gesture of defeat
(sound politics, I thought),
I washed these loving
histrionic hands.

The crowd surprised me, seized
the guilt of their demands.

                    You know
I am not weak. I could, I would
stand up for Jesus if I thought
that were the thing to do. Now
he is dead. He didn't seem to care,
so why should you? How is your head,
my sweet?

Joseph of Arimathaea

Sometimes, avoiding trouble, we accept defeat.
(Painful sometimes, being discreet.)

Soon Sabbath now. The corpse of Christ
ought to come down by then.
Which means pulling strings again.
I think I'll bury him where I
had planned to have my own bones lie.

Thank God, there's something I can do.
Forgive me, Lord, for not proclaiming you.

Swimmer

I

That powerful swimmer
furrowing the pool
towards the final wall. . .

II

Morn him, the crumpled athlete:
his element was water;
now they'll sink him
in the ground, he's gone
to rust, that muscled plough.

Give T'anks

Anodda year of love.
Give t'anks. An' pray
dat God-Above
will seh to time, No way,
No way:
de word is love.

The Day My Father Died

The day my father died
I could not cry;
My mother cried,
Not I.

His face on the pillow
In the dim light
Wrote mourning to me,
Black and white.

We saw him struggle,
Stiffen, relax;
The face fell empty,
Dead as wax.

I'd read of death
But never seen.
My father's face, I swear,
Was not serene;

Topple that lie,
However appealing:
That face was absence
Of all feeling.

My mother's tears were my tears,
Each sob shook me:
The pain of death is living,
The dead are free.

For me my father's death
Was mother's sorrow;
That day was her day,
Loss was tomorrow.

Philip Nanton

I

Where sea and land meet, begin there.
The ampersand, the join, is a fault
which caused jagged peaks to rise —
from the ocean's floor —
spanning a vacant gulf.
On any map of the world they are footnotes
reminders of nature's force.

Long ago, nomads, fragile as their pottery,
skimming waves, trecking from south to north,
stopped once too often for wood and water
and perished.
From the pre-ceramic Cibony
to the ceramics of Saladoid and Suazoid
we know them by their shards.
Common island caribs, sunk in a murderous tide
that flowed from east to west
bearing assassins and poets
the discoverers of the New World.

Come nearer, focus on one dot of an island
I was born there, on the rim of a volcano
on the edge of a large full stop
where the sand is black
where the hills turn a gun-barrel blue
where the sea perpetually dashes at the shoreline
trying to reclaim it all.

Grace Nichols

Wherever I Hang

I leave me people, me land, me home
For reasons, I not too sure
I forsake de sun
And de humming-bird splendour
Had big rats in de floorboard
So I pick up me new-world-self
And come, to this place call England
At first I feeling like I in dream –
De misty greyness
I touching de walls to see if they real
They solid to de seam
And de people pouring from de underground system
Like beans
And when I look up to de sky
I see Lord Nelson high – too high to lie

And is so I sending home photos of myself
Among de pigeons and de snow
And is so I warding off de cold
And is so, little by little
I begin to change my calypso ways
Never visiting nobody
Before giving them clear warning
And waiting me turn in queue
Now, after all this time
I get accustom to de English life
But I still miss back-home side
To tell you de truth
I don't know really where I belaang

  Yes, divided to de ocean
  Divided to de bone

Wherever I hang me knickers – that's my home.

Tropical Death

The fat black woman want
a brilliant tropical death
not a cold sojourn
in some North Europe far/forlorn

The fat black woman want
some heat/hibiscus at her feet
blue sea dress
to wrap her neat

The fat black woman want
some bawl
no quiet jerk tear wiping
a polite hearse withdrawal

The fat black woman want
all her dead rights
first night
third night
nine night
all the sleepless droning
red-eyed wake nights

In the heart
of her mother's sweetbreast
In the shade
of the sun leaf's cool bless
In the bloom
of her people's bloodrest

the fat black woman want
a brilliant tropical death yes

Sugar Cane

I

There is something
about sugarcane

he isn't what
he seem —

indifferent, hard
and sheathed in blades

his waving arms
is a sign for help

his skin thick
only to protect
the juice inside
himself

2

His colour
is the aura
of jaundice
when he ripe

he shiver
like ague
when it rain

he suffer
from bellywork
burning fever
and delirium

just before
the hurricane
strike
smashing him to pieces

3

Growing up
is an art

he don't have
any control of

it is us
who groom and
weed him

who stick him
in the earth
in the first place

and when he
growing tall

with the help
of the sun
and rain

we feel the
need to strangle
the life

out of him

But either way he can't survive

4

He cast his shadow
to the earth

the wind is
his only mistress

I hear them
moving
in rustling tones

she shakes
his hard reserve

smoothing
stroking
caressing
all his length
shamelessly

I crouch
below them
quietly

Epilogue

I have crossed an ocean
I have lost my tongue
from the root of the old one
a new one has sprung

Tapestry

— with Identity

The long line of blood
and family ties

An African countenance here
A European countenance there
An Amerindian cast of cheek
An Asianic turn of eye
And the tongue's salty accommodation
The tapestry is mine
All the bloodstained prints
The scatterlinks
The grafting strand of crinkled hair
The black persistent blooming.

Sasenarine Persaud

Rain Storm

This rage of waterangels
On zinc
Occurs when clouds touch
River.

The rotten gutter spews
Disintegrating jets
Of silver water
Crystal spinning droplets

Into the
Murky river
Bares her frothy
Underwear at thunder touch.

There is God and
You
In every drop
And droplet
Every liquid touch
And touchlet
Every streak of lightning
And every slap of thunder

Sees you and God
And I
Melt into each other.

Velma Pollard

Belize Suite

I   Sea Wall

Only a gentle swish
Where waves would touch the land
no wind no turbulence
along this wall arranged by man
dividing land from sea

No cruise-ships light this harbour end to end
only that cluster
where the army lights
ride there at anchor. . .
cool darkness and deluding calm

houses sit silent near the water's edge
their calm precarious like our peace
hoisted on stilts
like mokojumbies in the carnival
listening the ocean's gentle murmur
hearing its angry wail
what seems like decades now
when death rode loud and furious
on the hissing waves

From storm and earthquake Lord
deliver us
and us
and us

II   Xunantunich   (for Roy W)

The gods will ask
tell them I left my offering there
three handspans to the left
of that dread corner where the two slabs meet
under a stone
set in a threadbag
that I kept between my breasts
so that my hands could help me
timid goat
climb half way up
no more

it isn't strength that matters
courage to climb
is what the old hearts lose
my children's children never now will know
what sights the high-priests saw
undizzied by the dizzying heights

Power is always from on high
lookouts where pirates guard the harbour
rivers that tumble down from angry hills
cloud tops for cherubim
and Maya priests' Xunantunich

III   Road from Xunantunich

Dusk settles in
first near the edge
where towns like pale mirages sit
and only slowly shrouds us
shocked to silence by the stillness here. . .

Where are the night sounds
that begin at dusk?
not here or just not yet?

King trees with long and hairless trunks
reach green and fertile locks
towards the sky

no mountains here
no rocks
no green between those thick locks
and the close cropped kinks
that can't protect the land
cracked now with long unsightly breaks
(the geolog unstraps his EYE and clicks)

Who would be king
but with no subjects
who would grow strong and perfect
but alone?

This silence sobers us
and sends us feverish
seeking home

Su Su

Susu su su   Susu su su
among the yellow poui
you hear
I hear
leaves in the Japanese garden
'tiday fi mi tumaro fi yu'
like Brer Anancy talking in his nose
Susu su su

And how I laughed that day
I heard them say
'im shouldn bury there
im a go come back fi dem have no fear'
denying all the rural wisdom I had known. . .

Then quick and fast
some hidden hit man
strikes us off our anxious lists
and you
and I
stand open-mouthed
as poui leaves whisper just before they fall

tiday fi mi
tumaro fi yu
Susu su su
Susu su su

Victor Questel

Judge Dreadword

I am a murderer; I wring words by the rough of their necks,
I misplace commas and abuse silent W's. I use folk-
lift to get from one idea to the next.

I stab thoughts at people without
first preparing them by word of mouth.
I have language in a vice all my own. But today,
I appear before the country's chief judge and word protector:

Judge Dreadword. Yes I. Confess your atrocious crimes
to this Word Court. I am Judge Dreadword – I don't
brook silence in my court.

You are accused of lynching the word 'money' by
its second syllable; you violated a full-stop, you
stabbed three vowels when they weren't

looking. You exploded a bomb in the face of two
young phonemes. You copulated with the letters P and Y
. . . these acts make me blue

with rage, and I'm a hard man. I deal with your kind
every day. How do you plead Rude boy Q?
Guilty or not guilty? What should I do?

Not guilty sir. Take four hundred years. We must rid
society of your kind – insensitive word merchants like you
must be punished. You have no tradition, no lineage, no big

models. Don't write in this court. Take another two
hundred years. Rude boy Q have you heard of Johnson,
Cavafy, Eliot, Whitman, Lorca, Pasternak, Mandelstam?

Li Po? No your Dreadness. I thought so; a mere literary shim-
  sham.
Don't cry. This court is a product of a proven tradition
of oil and its related cultural benefactors —

BP, CIA, IMF, IOU, the UN, PNM — letters that matter
in the world. You want to destroy all that? Hush up.
I hear you detractors harbour vile thoughts against

foreign socio-linguists and visiting psycho-linguists — you
draw crude lop-side effigies of Chomsky, you hunt and burn
the manifestos of British dialectologists and American politicians.

You dare to write letters to the press. Don't interrupt,
I heard you were tough, but you snivel in my court.
Take another four hundred years. How dare you corrupt

our language? Why don't you dot your i's? Don't talk, I
do all the talking here. This is my court. Leave me.
Court is adjourned. Nail him to the cross of a T.

The Bush

You are in the bush;
the thicket of things. Frogs
spread the word and

mosquitoes bite whenever they can.
Now,
away from the harsh glare of rock,
the sting of green
burns the eye.

You can't masquerade in the bush;
it has its own rules. Strip to
the waist and wade through
a tangle of vines.

Men have been doing this since
the beginning of time – clearing
their minds of the bush
by entering its pain –

hacking backwards to the first tree or thorn.

Quietly the bush swallows the cut path.

Near Mourning Ground

Print tightened beneath candle grease like the drum-head
of memory
as uncle swirled suddenly to balance a point on
time
to the bell's appeal

as his eyes caught the staring shaking
brown robed whirl of my Spiritual Mother's
surrender
to Jordan
river.

She drew her shoulder blades together
rolled her lips,
noised a fit
and cut clean across the night air
of Curepe's oyster vendors,
coconut buyers
club-drinkers
and Maracas late-night travellers:

'Remember brethren to render
the tings that are Caesar's
to Caesar

and the tings that are God's . . .'

A child's hand slowly picked his nose
as he looked at the brass jar of leaves
and flowers planted on the
ground

as the Mother's eyes did not see apocalypse
though Shepherd, my uncle
had seen her private vision,
privately.

See uncle with red sash girdling his loins,
feet concrete hard scraping the cement
as he preached
the eyes tired but earnest

his truth riding as truth does
between poles of belief, the day's task
at shed five on the wharf still hard upon his back
though
soft candle, aloes and water-
cress had done their best to make him
shed that pain

to preach about the Lord's.

Uncle delivered not a vision or a dream
but a text
mounted from the lost books of the Bible

calmly prepared the night before by the arc
of the kerosene lamp;
and the sisters beneath the street
lamp approved as Shepherd's crook
hooked
a few wayward souls

to the song,
'At the cross, at the cross where I first
saw the light . . .'

as uncle remembered the private vision
and the public pain,
the heat and fears
the stoning of the brethren.

Though flesh is weak,
persecution and the retreat to the bush
never choked their voices,

they had learnt that here
it was more important to confront
Jordan river than to cross it.

But Shepherd is like any writer
here,
a lonely pilgrim going to meet himself
a man burning on mourning ground

grounded by a vision of flight and travel
heat
and fears

weekend baptisms,
constantly trying to cross water
fasting
eyes covered by several colours of seeing
reduced,

returned and returning to the blank
page
trying to speak the vision clearly
though he cannot
without a text.

Listen uncle as the sisters hum us home,
what tract yer pull,
traveller,
mourner
man at the cross roads

after your years of aloes,
cutting through the creeping vines of age
hearing your parables of delivery
watching the bell-bottoms ringing out
a truth that leaves you sitting tight
sensing only laughter, heat and fears?

Lord uncle say the word.

And uncle preaching since the time the Yankees leave the base.

Rajandaye Ramkissoon-Chen

Father

Daylight cranked the start of work.
The ricemill throbbed with life
And,
My father's mind rolled
With the mill's flat belt.

His measure was the pitch-oil-tin.
Each one, paddy-filled
My father heaved in-
to the mill's high funnel.

The milled rice, white,
Ran down the spout
Like the stitches on his kurtah hem,
Yellow paddy shells converting
To gold studs for its neck.

Beneath the house
Was the depository for husk.
We piled hillocks
Wide
And to the flooring top.
With buckets in hand
Like little Hillarys we climbed.
We dug footprints
Into savings
For the arid times.

I once sold rice husk
The jute bags grew
Over my head.
I pressed my mind
Like a calulator
And displayed the figures
In pennies and cents.

The muffler once snorted
Sparks and smoke
Over dried-leaf eddies
Little brass-plates
Doing a Hindu *aarti*.

A pitchyard thrust back
Our home.
Paddy dried like nuggets
In the sun.
Animals standing
And awaiting their loads
splashed in the yard
Bullion-lumps of dung.
Raleigh, here,
Would have found together
Both his La Brea and
The City of Manoa.

When the Hindu Woman Sings Calypso

The moon takes on the glint of sun
Sleep flies, eyelids open
Legs supine rise to rhythm,
Past the midnight.

There, where she was born
In those early days
The village lamplight
With the cock's last crow
Was out. Feet huddled
Fast in sleep.

Strings of rhinestone now
'*Purdah*' her forehead
Her hair is frizzled
To a '*Buss-up-shot*'
The long tresses of
A long tradition
Seared in the electricity
Of the mike's cord length.

The glare of stage-lights
Takes over the backyard.
There was her training
Near standpipe and river.
That was the ground where only
Girls and women danced
To '*tassa*' drummings
Of pre-nuptial celebrations

Her song resounds, her
Hips gyrate, knees bend.
Her trousers balloon
Like a rich-clad Mogul's
Their shimmer sliced
Their folds open.

Her midriff's bare
Looped white with pearls
Her body sinuous
With the dance of muscle.
She stoops as for a *'limbo'* number
Head held backward from the rod-fire.
Leaves of flame
Play on her bodice.

Her voice vibrates
Past stage to audience,
Through all transmissions
The whole country listens
Night insects, they too
Stop their churrings
As she sings and *'winds'*
To calypso and *'pan'*
With a *'tassa'* blending.

Andrew Salkey

Inside

Time and again,
she had been carelessly used,
hurt, pulped
and spat out by her friends.

She put the pain of the years
in her cupped hands,
looked at it hard
and tried to squeeze it
tight and dry:
but she failed.

The anguish bunched.
It burst through the slits
of her fingers
and stung her eyes,
just as the pinched rind
often did
in her mother's kitchen.

She sits, now,
her hands smelling of limes,
and tries to work out
what went wrong
with all those early
close relationships,
how things got more
and more twisted and snarled,
what caused the dislocation
and the drift,

what made her so rootedly trusting;
and she knows
that she is not alone to blame.

A certain pinking process,
set in motion, long ago,
had done the trick,
had turned the earth
and geared the growth.

Lime trees still grow
in her mother's garden,
next to the kitchen,
and the pain simply won't subside.

Away

For Charles Hyatt

I hold a banyan of memories of home
in my head; I have a Rio Bueno of slides:
an unbroken flow of air mail envelopes,
their zig-zag borders carrying on and on,
until the unseen sender returned and died;
someone else, just as faithful, a Harriet
who stayed beside me but who also died;
a large dining-room blackboard on which
singular verb matched singular subject;
that end-and-beginning-of-the-year Swift ham,
brown with sugar and jabbed black with cloves;
the slow, slow understanding of '38;
those very painful examination years;
the inconsolable lack of a community bell;
abeng, broken again and again, and discarded;

the lizard on its back; the waste of men;
the long line of women at the bottom of the hill;
the warmth that goes for nothing; the lies;
the story no leader will tell; the drift;
the blaze of poinsettias; the sunset at sunrise;
the burning image of West Kingston as hell.

The voices in my room say something, perhaps
nothing at all that really means anything.
And yet, they persist. They claim they have a way
with history, with all the people who make it.
Meanwhile, the everlasting banyan spiders the earth
and slowly penetrating Rio Bueno flows and flows.

A Song for England

An a so de rain a-fall
An a so de snow a-rain

An a so de fog a-fall
An a so de sun a-fail

An a so de seasons mix
An a so de bag-o-tricks

But a so me understan
De misery o de Englishman.

Dennis Scott

Marrysong

He never learned her, quite. Year after year
that territory, without seasons, shifted
under his eye. An hour he could be lost
in the walled anger of her quarried hurt
on turning, see cool water laughing where
the day before there were stones in her voice.
He charted. She made wilderness again.
Roads disappeared. The map was never true.
Wind brought him rain sometimes, tasting of sea —
and suddenly she would change the shape of shores
faultlessly calm. All, all was each day new:
the shadows of her love shortened or grew
like trees seen from an unexpected hill,
new country at each jaunty helpless journey.
So he accepted that geography, constantly strange.
Wondered. Stayed home increasingly to find
his way among the landscapes of her mind.

Apocalypse dub

At first, there's a thin, bright Rider –
he doesn't stop at the supermarket, the cool
red meats are not to his taste.
He steals from the tin on the tenement table,
he munches seed from the land
where no rain has fallen, he feeds
in the gutter behind my house.
The bread is covered with sores
when he eats it; the children
have painted his face on their bellies

The second rides slowly, is visiting, watch him, he smiles
through the holes in the roof
of the cardboard houses.
His exhaust sprays pus on the sheets,
he touches the women and teaches them
fever, he puts eggs under the skin –
in the hot days insects will hatch and hide
in the old men's mouths,
in the bones of the children

And always, behind them, the iceman, quick,
with his shades, the calm oil of his eyes –
when he throttles, the engine
grunts like a killer. I'm afraid,
you said. Then you closed the window
and turned up the radio, the DJ said greetings
to all you lovely people.
But in the street the children coughed like guns.

In the blueblack evenings
they cruise on the corner
giggling. Skenneng! Skenneng!

Dreadwalk

for the Children

blackman came walking I
heard him sing his
voice was like sand
when the wind dries it

said sing for me dreamer
said blackman I cannot
the children are gone
like sand from the quarry

said are you afraid I
come closer said blackman
his teeth were like stone
where the pick cuts it

said do you remember
my mouth full of stones he said
give I the children
would not step aside

but you holding it wrong I
said love the fist opened
the knife fell away from
the raw hand middle

his voice was like wind
when the sea makes it salt
the sun turned a little
the shadows rolled flat
blowing closer afaid I
would not step aside

then he held me into
his patience   locked

one

now I sing for the children
like wind in the quarry
hear me now
by the wide torn places

I am walking

Epitaph

They hanged him on a clement morning, swung
between the falling sunlight and the women's
breathing, like a black apostrophe to pain.
All morning while the children hushed
their hopscotch joy and the cane kept growing
he hung there sweet and low.
                              At least that's how
they tell it. It was long ago
and what can we recall of a dead slave or two
except that when we punctuate our island tale
they swing like sighs across the brutal
sentences, and anger pauses
till they pass away.

Olive Senior

Birdshooting Season

Birdshooting season the men
make marriages with their guns
My father's house turns macho
as from far the hunters gather

All night long contentless women
stir their brews: hot coffee
chocolata, cerassie
wrap pone and tie-leaf
for tomorrow's sport. Tonight
the men drink white rum neat.

In darkness shouldering
their packs, their guns, they leave

We stand quietly on the
doorstep shivering. Little boys
longing to grow up birdhunters too
Little girls whispering:
Fly Birds Fly.

Searching for Grandfather

I

In Colón I searched for my
grandfather without connection.
Not even the message of his
name in the phone book.

II

Along the Line I found my
grandfather disconnected
at Culebra
            Hacking at the Cut
he coughed his brains loose
and shook

(but it was only malaria)

You're lucky they said as they
shipped him home on the deck
of a steamer, his mind
fractured but his fortune intact:
Twenty-eight dollars and two
cents. Silver.

III

What he had learnt to do really
well in Colón was wash corpses.
At home the village was too poor
to patronise. He was the one
that died.

His sisters laid him out in a
freshly-made coffin and cried:
there was nothing left of the
Silver Roll to weigh down his
eyes.

For although his life had been
lacking in baggage, they didn't
want him to see that on this
voyage out he still travelled
steerage.

To the Madwoman in my Yard

Lady: please don't throw rocks at my window
because this is Holy House and God send you
to get all the moneylenders out drive the harlot
from the inner temple. Again. Please don't
creep up behind me when I'm gardening beg me
lend you a knife. A bucket. A rope. Hope. Then
threaten to ignite, set alight and consume me
for you are the Daughter-of-a-Eunuch-and-a-Firefly
sent to X-ray and exhume me.

Lady: this is nonsense. Here I am trying hard
with my Life. With Society. You enter my yard
dressed like furies or bats. Bring right in to me
all the hell I've been trying to escape from.
Thought a Barbican gate could hold in the
maelstrom. Keep out the Dungle. And bats.

What you want? Bring me down to your level?
— A life built on scraps. A fretwork of memory
which is garbage. A jungle of images: parson
and hellfire all that's sustaining. The childhood
a house built of straw could not stand. The man
like a roach on the walls. So you choose
out of doors. Or my garden.

Lady: as you rant and you shout, threaten
and cajole me, seek me out then debar me
you don't move me one blast: Life Equals Control.

Yes. Here is what the difference between us
is about: I wear my madness in. You wear yours out.

Hill Country

The sun etches out the minutes of my days
under my dark eyes. The train, our only
regulation, shakes down the hours stakes out
the limits of our lives
on this, my harsh and gentle island.

My ring finger tingles as my machete
flints on a stone. From far
hear my wife pounding cassava
in a cracked mortar singing
a cracked tune O
                              the futility
of crop cultivation in this place
the census takers never come. To whom
shall I marry my daughter?

Sons, too young to help, too old
to be not-born, too precious
to have seedlings feeding on your dreams
Fist this red clay in your hands
hold the red gold, I tell them.
But I look into their eyes
and no gold comes, no dreams
arise and I know
this is merely the red clay
of a broken hillside and the parakeets
sit on the cedar stump waiting
for the young corn to ripen.

The sun cuts an arc on the housetop
the day goes by
my thoughts tremble on the edge
of something undesirable
my wife sings still
the sunbaked questions
of our lives . . .

The sun marks the minutes, the train
the hours. Among the yam vines
and the trumpet trees we need
no clocks, no timepieces, no time
for the hunger in our bellies tells us
which way a clock's hands should go.

The train pulls home the day
draws it into citylights on two
black parallels. Later
when my sons discover the agonies
of leached hillsides
it will draw them too
                              O weigh
down these memories
with a stone.

Children's Hospital

Look now the child
facing death. Who
will commute this sentence
to life?

A. J. Seymour

Name Poem

Beauty about us in the breathe of names
Known to us all, but murmured over softly
Woven to breath of peace.

If but a wind blows, all their beauty wakes.

Kwebanna on the Waini — Indian words
And peace asleep within the syllables.

Cabacaburi and the Rupununi
Reverence is guest in that soft hush of names.

For battle music and the roll of drums.
The shock and break of bodies locked in combat
The Tramen Cliff above Imbaimadai.

Guiana, Waini are cousin water words . . .

The Demerary, Desakepe and Courantyne
Flow centuries before strange tongues bewitch
Their beauty into common county names.

Through all the years before the Indians came
Rocks at Tumatumari kept their grace,
And Tukeit, Amatuk and Waratuk
Trained ear and eye for thundering Kaieteur.

And there are mountain tops that take the sun
Jostling shoulders with seaward-eyed Roraima . . .

These Amerindian names hold ancient sway
Beyond the European fingers reaching,
Forever reaching in, but nearer coast
Words born upon Dutch tongues live in our speech.

The sentinel that was Kykoveral
Beterverwagting, Vlissengen and Stabroek
And sonorous toll of bells in Vergenoegen.

For French remembrance, Le Ressouvenir,
The silent and great tomb of an exile's anguish,
Le Repentir – that city of the dead . . .

Simple the heritage of English names
Hid in Adventure, Bee Hive, Cove and John,
And Friendship, Better Hope, and Land of Canaan
Garden of Eden and . . . so Paradise.

Out west are places blessed by Spanish tongues
Santa Rosa, white chapel on a hill . . .

Beauty about us in the breathe of names,
If but a wind blows, all their beauty wakes.

To The Family Home Awaiting Repair

Oh, long narrow home heavy with living
An age of memories people the walls
Around your naked frame.

Warm shell of love & crowding children
Where the young girls in uniform
Hats worn like horseguards
Speech full of the school diction
Cycle up to ask for who's at home.

And the cool Trade Winds carry echoes
Pavan for A Dead Princess
Played on the Thorens
Until it wore the grooves.

The scent of roses in the slim garden
Growing in the four-hour overhead sun
Smell of bread from the oven
Everything mingling in the wind.

The tales we told around the dining table
Linking the luncheons with their spell
(Sometimes the battlefield for table tennis).

The statue of JT at the desk
Image of the dedicated student.
The stairs are torn away that quivered to the steps
Impatient for games & parties but slow for school.

So many came here – tea-visiting professors,
Exam students, poets, novelists, sculptors,
A Chief Justice – a future Prime Minister
Once talked halfway through the night.

Through a hole in the hooded verandah
The bats spelt six o'clock evening patrol.

And little children to the Kindergarden
Wrestling their way into the hall of learning
Chattering, tormenting the wild cherry-tree
That always yields its fruit.

Oh, crowd your long years of memory
Into a prayer for their future
For all who lived and loved and studied here.

Millionaire

I have written a million words,
Life-long a single poem,
In my hallelujah chorus.

Celebrating the skipping boy
Girl flaunting her curving beauty
The old man shuffling along
The leaf with the rain on it.

Celebrating my human tree,
The memories that whisper of childhood
And its care-free happiness

My memory, nameless and vast,
Pushes roots in the nation's past
And the past coming leaping to life,
Defying time to print
The black velvet of my mind.

The happy cascading bells
Trembling in songs of joy
A crystal contains them all.

The tilapia in the trench
Burrow deep in a cave of mud
Fancying themselves to be safe,
From fingers impregnable

But the secrets, dark in the heart
Yield their jewels at harvest time,
The creative imagination.

Jonathan Small

Pig-sticking Season

The pig swelled in the sun
drum-tight, feet like avenging arrows.
You couldn't want a deader pig
than this. The egret knew it,
adopting a proprietary pose.
All afternoon it stood
unshaken by the wind.
Once, a wing unfolded
stretched with custodial care,
the page of a book solemnly closing.

This season scavengers are gathering
in increasing numbers
near city morgues. Each hamlet
daily loses faith in the familiar stench;
grows more cannibalistic.
No one bothers to count the dead.
News bulletins say the morgues are crowded
with unclaimed bodies. That's not all.
Municipal employees have gone home again.
What happens when collection is called off?

In this pig-sticking season
ambulances scream through barricades of trash;
teeth shiver, set on edge in too-bright sun.
No one knows whose daughter
will be gunned down next,
whose mother will turn whore

by the crude collusion of political sweet-talk,
auctions and lay-offs. The thin gloves
of democracy sweat handing irons to the poor.
Official chamber talks create a stink,
the worse because victor and victim
share the same black dream. You dare
to criticize Botha's regime!

Stick a pig and see it bleed;
hold celebrations before egrets strike
at the colossus called democracy.
Who drove the hag out of her village hut
will bruise the heels of children and exploit
a widow in her grief. Call it what you will.
I prefer pig-sticking.

Eating the Elephant Whole

Oliver, according to Tutu
there's only one way to eat an elephant –
one piece at a time.
You want to ambush it, spear it
and eat it whole. A lot of Zulus agree
with you too, but as time passes
it gets more difficult knowing where
to begin cutting off

the monolithic germ. You know it
Tambo, and all Soweto
waiting to light the elephant pot.
They're learning fast from you
to vocalise their spears
cutting off

worshippers of the Swedish prize
whose stinking mausoleum sweats
with ivory icons and tablets
marbled in old academic quarries.

But hear: Pretoria will rise
like the baked Phoenix at every skirmish
cutting off

all who arbitrate in ivory towers
to keep the earth's rotation neat.
Kill the beast and let your conscience
explode. Soweto's children must live
to see Mandela reach.
Death to the elephant!

Michael Smith

A Go Blow Fire

Me naw disown dis-ya talk
fi chat bout me freedom.
Naw tun criminal
siddung fill me lungs wid smoke
and sing song of lamentation
all day long.

Yuh tink every day I a go get up
an jus blow like dus
an when I cry
fi-I tears tun to pus?

I cyaan just a galang
a hope like a barren lan fi rain.
I soon bus

for behind I is darkness,
round I destruction,
an before I
hunger
a go blow fire!

Black and White

went to an all black school
with an all black name
all black principal
black teacher

graduated
with an all black concept

with our blackety blackety frustration
we did an all black march
with high black hopes
and an all black song

got a few solutions
not all black

went to a show
and saw our struggles
in black and white

Lawwwwwd have mercy

Dis-ya Dutty

Dis-ya dutty, a we create it
wid we sweat an we blood;
an we nourish it.

Fire come bun we,
water come wet we,
people come teck liberty
an step pon we;
ten cent, we no got i.

Dis-ya dutty, we hate it;
but at times
a it warm we.

Koo pon we:
we black but we no ugly.
Koo pon we:
come trace we history.

Revolutionary

Yuh see all de time
a siddung ya naw seh nutten?
A jus a tink
how a never have no fahder
an how a had to model me modder
fi live ina one little tenement yard
which part everybody tink dem better off
dan de odder, yet when night come
dem ben up like exercise book,
siddung a wonder wha dem a go cook.

She never business bout Africa,
much less fi go like Rasta,
an she woulda wuk night an day,
make sacrifice an pray.
For all she waan fi know,
dat her son come out to sinting better
so she can move outa de hog pen
an show off pon her frien.

I remember de fus day
de bull come inna de pen,
im seh, 'A goin ketch dis dungle a fire
an buil some concrete structure,
dat pon a dark day
yuh can stretch outside an polish de sky!'
An we seh dis was progress,
content wid an incompleteness
inside.

Now I tun man
I sight up a revolutionary vision:
if we waan seh roots any at all
we haffi go stop we mumma from movin
from yard to yard

Ralph Thompson

He knows what Height Is

He knows what height is, this hillside dweller
who squints occasionally at the waving sea
below, the lustre of its greener
eye engulfing the valley to return his gaze.
One day, hacking at high vines
he saw his cutlass hanging in the sky,
motionless, an off-course Air Jamaica
plane aimed at the airport. He has never
flown, assumes that those who do by looking down
can bless or cast a spell upon the ground.

High is the axed pine that pitches forward
shivering like a compass needle in the circle
of the clearing, pulled true north to where the bird,
a Solitaire, like him a mountain exile,
flutes its two-note elegy, centre
of lamentation in which his hut is huddled.
At dusk he slides down the slope from field
to shack, leaning back against the incline,
heels hugging dirt, a trickle of stones
rolling before him into the ravine.

He sits alone at sunset, the hills hunched
around him leaking purple, the black crack
of the gorge narrowing to a scar stitched
into the mountain's back. Clinging to the brink
of the precipice his hut is a wattled
blink of lantern light behind
the streaming banners of the evening mist.

Then suddenly the bird – a black silken
knot unravelling down the valley! Free,
it rocks on the scooped air. Then
as he knows it will, dips, followed by a
fury of ascent, arching up
contemptuous of gravity, swift
and pure as the crescent curve of his machete.
At another time, another edge, he watched
his mother climb a guinep tree, skirt
billowing in the breeze and from a limb
lower a swing for him, sisal knotted
under a wooden slat. Higher and higher
she pushed him into terrifying air.

The bird floats down the mountain, wings at rest,
riding high currents over the ridges, swinging
him between the peaks, feet dangling
above the abyss filling up with shadows,
elbows screaming at his sides,
fingers frozen on the fog frayed vines.
Gabriel or Lucifer? As
it was in the beginning so, after all
these years, the sign and wonder – between his legs
the anus closing, the shrinking of the balls.

Derek Walcott

'Midsummer LIV'

The midsummer sea, the hot pitch road, this grass, these shacks
    that made me,
jungle and razor grass shimmering by the roadside, the edge of
    art;
wood lice are humming in the sacred wood,
nothing can burn them out, they are in the blood;
their rose mouths, like cherubs, sing of the slow science
of dying – all heads, with, at each ear, a gauzy wing.
Up at Forest Reserve, before branches break into sea,
I looked through the moving, grassed window and thought
    'pines,'
or conifers of some sort. I thought, they must suffer
in this tropical heat with their child's idea of Russia.
Then suddenly, from their rotting logs, distracting signs
of the faith I betrayed, or the faith that betrayed me –
yellow butterflies rising on the road to Valencia
stuttering 'yes' to the resurrection; 'yes, yes is our answer,'
the gold-robed Nunc Dimittis of their certain choir.
Where's my child's hymnbook, the poems edged in gold leaf,
the heaven I worship with no faith in heaven,
as the Word turned toward poetry in its grief?
Ah, bread of life, that only love can leaven!
Ah, Joseph, though no man ever dies in his own country,
the grateful grass will grow thick from his heart.

The Season of Phantasmal Peace

Then all the nations of birds lifted together
the huge net of the shadows of this earth
in multitudinous dialects, twittering tongues,
stitching and crossing it. They lifted up
the shadows of long pines down trackless slopes,
the shadows of glass-faced towers down evening streets,
the shadow of a frail plant on a city sill –
the net rising soundless as night, the birds' cries soundless, until
there was no longer dusk, or season, decline, or weather,
only this passage of phantasmal light
that not the narrowest shadow dared to sever.

And men could not see, looking up, what the wild geese drew,
what the ospreys trailed behind them in silvery ropes
that flashed in the icy sunlight; they could not hear
battalions of starlings waging peaceful cries,
bearing the net higher, covering this world
like the vines of an orchard, or a mother drawing
the trembling gauze over the trembling eyes
of a child fluttering to sleep;
                                    it was the light
that you will see at evening on the side of a hill
in yellow October, and no one hearing knew
what change had brought into the raven's cawing,
the killdeer's screech, the ember-circling chough
such an immense, soundless, and high concern
for the fields and cities where the birds belong,
except it was their seasonal passing, Love,
made seasonless, or, from the high privilege of their birth,
something brighter than pity for the wingless ones
below them who shared dark holes in windows and in houses,
and higher they lifted the net with soundless voices
above all change, betrayals of falling suns,

and this season lasted one moment, like the pause
between dusk and darkness, between fury and peace,
but, for such as our earth is now, it lasted long.

Elsewhere

For Stephen Spender

Somewhere a white horse gallops with its mane
plunging round a field whose sticks
are ringed with barbed wire, and men
break stones or bind straw into ricks.

Somewhere women tire of the shawled sea's
weeping, for the fishermen's dories
still go out. It is blue as peace.
Somewhere they're tired of torture stories.

That somewhere there was an arrest.
Somewhere there was a small harvest
of bodies in the truck. Soldiers rest
somewhere by a road, or smoke in a forest.

Somewhere there is the conference rage
at an outrage. Somewhere a page
is torn out, and somehow the foliage
no longer looks like leaves but camouflage.

Somewhere there is a comrade,
a writer lying with his eyes wide open
on mattress ticking, who will not read
this, or write. How to make a pen?

And here we are free for a while, but
elsewhere, in one-third, or one-seventh
of this planet, a summary rifle butt
breaks a skull into the idea of a heaven

where nothing is free, where blue air
is paper-frail, and whatever we write
will be stamped twice, a blue letter,
its throat slit by the paper knife of the state.

Through these black bars
hollowed faces stare. Fingers
grip the cross bars of these stanzas
and it is here, because somewhere else

their stares fog into oblivion
thinly, like the faceless numbers
that bewilder you in your telephone
diary. Like last year's massacres.

The world is blameless. The darker crime
is to make a career of conscience,
to feel through our own nerves the silent scream
of winter branches, wonders read as signs.

The Hotel Normandie Pool

I

Around the cold pool in the metal light
of New Year's morning, I choose one of nine
cast-iron umbrellas set in iron tables
for work and coffee. The first cigarette
triggers the usual fusillade of coughs.
After a breeze the pool settles the weight
of its reflections on one line. Sunshine
lattices a blank wall with the shade of gables,
stirs the splayed shadows of the hills like moths.

Last night, framed in the binding of that window,
like the great chapter in some Russian novel
in which, during the war, the prince comes home
to watch the soundless waltzers dart and swivel,
like fishes in their lamplit aquarium,
I stood in my own gauze of swirling snow
and, through the parted hair of ribboned drapes,
felt, between gusts of music, the pool widen
between myself and those light-scissored shapes.

The dancers stiffened and, like fish, were frozen
in panes of ice blocked by the window frames;
one woman fanned, still fluttering on a pin,
as a dark fusillade of kettledrums
and a piercing cornet played 'Auld Lang Syne'
while a battalion of drunk married men
reswore their vows. For this my fiftieth year,
I muttered to the ribbon-medalled water,
'Change me, my sign, to someone I can bear.'

Now my pen's shadow, angled at the wrist
with the chrome stanchions at the pool's edge,
dims on its lines like birches in a mist
as a cloud fills my hand. A drop punctuates
the startled paper. The pool's iron umbrellas
ring with the drizzle. Sun hits the water.
The pool is blinding zinc. I shut my eyes,
and as I raise their lids I see each daughter
ride on the rayed shells of both irises.

The prayer is brief: That the transparent wrist
would not cloud surfaces with my own shadow,
and that this page's surface would unmist
after my breath as pools and mirrors do.
But all reflection gets no easier,
although the brown, dry needles of that palm
quiver to stasis and things resume their rhyme
in water, like the rubber ring that is a
red rubber ring inverted at the line's center.

Into that ring my younger daughter dived
yesterday, slithering like a young dolphin,
her rippling shadow hungering under her,
with nothing there to show how well she moved
but in my mind the veer of limb and fin.
Transparent absences! Love makes me look
through a clear ceiling into rooms of sand;
I ask the element that is my sign,
'Oh, let her lithe head through that surface break!'

Aquarian, I was married to water;
under that certain roof, I would lie still
next to my sister spirit, horizontal
below what stars derailed our parallel
from our far vow's undeviating course;
the next line rises as they enter it,
Peter, Anna, Elizabeth – Margaret
still sleeping with one arm around each daughter,
in the true shape of love, beyond divorce.

Time cuts down on the length man can endure
his own reflection. Entering a glass
I surface quickly now, prefer to breathe
the fetid and familiar atmosphere
of work and cigarettes. Only tyrants believe
their mirrors, or Narcissi, brooding on boards,
before they plunge into their images;
at fifty I have learnt that beyond words
is the disfiguring exile of divorce.

II

Across blue seamless silk, iron umbrellas
and a brown palm burn. A sandalled man comes out
and, in a robe of foam-frayed terry cloth,
with Roman graveness buries his room key,
then, mummy-oiling both forearms and face
with sunglasses still on, stands, fixing me,
and nods. Some petty businessman who tans
his pallor a negotiable bronze,
and the bright nod would have been commonplace

as he uncurled his shades above the pool's
reflecting rim – white towel, toga-slung,
foam hair repeated by the robe's frayed hem –
but, in the lines of his sun-dazzled squint,
a phrase was forming in that distant tongue
of which the mind keeps just a mineral glint,
the lovely Latin lost to all our schools:
'*Quis te misit, Magister?*' And its whisper went
through my cold body, veining it in stone.

On marble, concrete, or obsidian,
your visit, Master, magnifies the lines
of our small pool to that Ovidian
thunder of surf between the Baltic pines.
The light that swept Rome's squares and palaces,
washing her tangled fountains of green bronze
when you were one drop in a surf of faces –
a fleck of spittle from the she-wolf's tooth –
now splashes a palm's shadow at your foot.

Turn to us, Ovid. Our emerald sands
are stained with sewage from each tin-shacked Rome;
corruption, censorship, and arrogance
make exile seem a happier thought than home.
'Ah, for the calm proconsul with a voice
as just and level as this Roman pool,'
our house slaves sigh; the field slaves scream revenge;
one moves between the flatterer and the fool
yearning for the old bondage from both ends.

And I, whose ancestors were slave and Roman,
have seen both sides of the imperial foam,
heard palm and pine tree alternate applause
as the white breakers rose in galleries
to settle, whispering at the tilted palm
of the boy-god Augustus. My own face
held negro Neros, chalk Caligulas;
my own reflection slid along the glass
of faces foaming past triumphal cars.

Master, each idea has become suspicious
of its shadow. A lifelong friend whispers
in his own house as if it might arrest him;
markets no more applaud, as was their custom,
our camouflaged, booted militias
roaring past on camions, the sugar-apples
of grenades growing on their belts; ideas
with guns divide the islands; in dark squares
the poems gather like conspirators.

Then Ovid said, 'When I was first exiled,
I missed my language as your tongue needs salt,
in every watery shape I saw my child,
no bench would tell my shadow "Here's your place";
bridges, canals, willow-fanned waterways
turned from my parting gaze like an insult,
till, on a tablet smooth as the pool's skin,
I made reflections that, in many ways,
were even stronger than their origin.

'Tiled villas anchored in their foaming orchards,
parched terraces in a dust cloud of words,
among clod-fires, wolfskins, starving herds,
Tibullus' flute faded, sweetest of shepherds.
Through shaggy pines the beaks of needling birds
pricked me at Tomis to learn their tribal tongue,
so, since desire is stronger than its disease,
my pen's beak parted till we chirped one song
in the unequal shade of equal trees.

'Campaigns enlarged our frontiers like clouds,
but my own government was the bare boards
of a plank table swept by resinous pines
whose boughs kept skittering from Caesar's eye
with every yaw. There, hammering out lines
in that green forge to fit me for the horse,
I bent on a solitude so tyrannous
against the once seductive surf of crowds
that no wife softens it, or Caesar's envy.

'And where are those detractors now who said
that in and out of the imperial shade
I scuttled, showing to a frowning sun
the fickle dyes of the chameleon?
Romans' – he smiled – 'will mock your slavish rhyme,
the slaves your love of Roman structures, when,
from Metamorphoses to Tristia,
art obeys its own order. Now it's time.'
Trying his toga gently, he went in.

There, at the year's horizon, he had stood,
as if the pool's meridian were the line
that doubled the burden of his solitude
in either world; and, as one leaf fell,
his echo rippled: 'Why here, of all places,
a small, suburban tropical hotel,
its pool pitched to a Mediterranean blue,
its palms rusting in their concrete oasis?
Because to make my image flatters you.'

III

At dusk, the sky is loaded like watercolour paper
with an orange wash in which every edge frays—
a painting with no memory of the painter—
and what this proof recites is not a phrase
from an invisible, exiled laureate,
where there's no laurel, but the scant applause
of one dry, scraping palm tree as blue eve-
ning ignites its blossoms from one mango flower,
and something, not a leaf, falls like a leaf,

as swifts with needle-beaks dart, panicking over
the pool's cloud-closing light. For an envoi,
write what the wrinkled god repeats to the boy-
god. 'May the last light of heaven pity us
for the hardening lie in the face that we did not tell.'
Dusk. The trees blacken like the pool's umbrellas.
Dusk. Suspension of every image and its voice.
The mangoes pitch from their green dark like meteors.
The fruit bat swings on its branch, a tongueless bell.

BIOGRAPHICAL NOTES

Where dates of birth are known they are included. Several poets declined to provide this information on the grounds that it is irrelevant.

John Agard (Guyana) b. 1949; poet, performer and children's author who has been living in the UK since 1977. His books include *Man to Pan* (Casa de las Americas, 1982), *Mangoes and Bullets* and *Lovelines for a Goat-Born Lady* (both Serpent's Tail, 1990). He reads a selection of his work on the *Bluefoot Cassettes* and the anthology discs *An Evening of International Poetry* and *Come From That Window Child* (details p 236).

Edward Baugh (Jamaica) b. 1936; best known as a critic, teacher and professor in the Dept of English, University of the West Indies, Jamaica. He is the author of many critical articles and studies, including *Derek Walcott: Memory as Vision: Another Life* (Longman, 1978). His poetry has been widely published in journals and anthologies and collected in *A Tale From The Rain Forest* (Sandberry Press, 1988).

Louise Bennett (Jamaica) b. 1919; writer, performer and broadcaster. One of the pivotal figures of twentieth century Caribbean literature, her books include *Jamaica Labrish* (Sangsters, 1966) and *Selected Poems* ed. Mervyn Morris (Sangsters, 1982). Several records and cassettes of her work are available, including *Yes M'Dear* (Island Records) and *Miss Lou's Views*.

James Berry (Jamaica) b. 1924; has lived in the US and, since 1945, in the UK. Following publication of his first collection, *Fractured Circles* (New Beacon Books, 1979), his work has flourished. He edited two important anthologies of West Indian-British poetry, *Bluefoot Traveller* (Harrap, 1981) and *News for Babylon* (Chatto Poetry, 1984). His most recent collections include *Chain of Days* (OUP, 1975) and *When I Dance* (Hamish Hamilton, 1988). He reads a selection of his work on the *Bluefoot Cassettes* (details p 236), which he edited.

Edward Kamau Brathwaite (Barbados) b. 1930; poet, historian, critic, editor and bibliographer. Until recently he taught in the Dept of History at the University of the West Indies, Jamaica, but he now teaches at New York University. His poetry collections include *The Arrivants* (OUP, 1981), *Masks* (Nexus Books, 1981), *Mother Poem* (OUP, 1977), *Sun Poem* (OUP, 1982), *X/SELF* (OUP, 1987), and *Middle Passages* (Blood-axe, 1992). A five-disc set of his reading of the *Arrivants* trilogy was issued by Argo in the 1970s. The Association of Teachers of African and Caribbean Literature issued a cassette of a workshop on *Mother Poem* that he gave in the early '80s and the British Council issued a cassette of

Brathwaite speaking about his work and reading from *Masks*. He also reads on the *Poets of the West Indies* disc (details p 236).

Jean Binta Breeze (Jamaica) trained at the Jamaica School of Drama and was a teacher of English and Drama before becoming a full-time writer. She has won international acclaim for her dub poetry and her performances and she has recently been working in film and television. Her publications include the collections *Answers* (Mansini Productions, 1983), *Riddym Ravings* (Race Today Publications 1988) and *Spring Cleaning* (Virago, 1992). She has made several recordings of her work, including *Riddym Ravings* (Reachout International Records, 1987).

Wayne Brown (Trinidad and Tobago) b. 1944; poet, critic, journalist and university teacher. His first collection *On The Coast* (Andre Deutsch, 1972) won the Commonwealth Poetry Prize and a second collection, *Voyages* (Inprint Caribbean), came out in 1989. He has also published a beautiful biography of Edna Manley and edited a schools edition of Derek Walcott's poetry. A collection of his stories and essays, *The Child of the Sea* (Inprint Caribbean) was published in 1990.

Jan Carew (Guyana) b. 1920; presently Emeritus Professor of African American and Third World Studies of Northwestern University and Visiting Professor of International Studies at Illinois Wesleyan University. Perhaps best known for his three novels published in the late '50s and early '60s, *Black Midas, The Wild Coast* and *The Last Barbarian*. Other publications include two children's books and a collection of poems, *Sea Drums in My Blood* (New Voices, Trinidad, 1981).

Martin Carter (Guyana) b. 1927; one of the region's major poets, his reputation was founded on his early *Poems of Resistance* (Lawrence & Wishart, 1954) written out of his experience in the anti-colonial struggle in Guyana, during which he was imprisoned for a time. He was subsequently a Minister of Culture in a post-independence government but in recent years has been Writer in Residence at the University of Guyana. The poems of four decades are represented in his *Selected Poems* (Demerara Publications, 1989).

Brian Chan (Guyana) b. 1942; a musician and painter, he now lives in Alberta, Canada. In 1988 he published a collection of poems, *Thief With Leaf* (Peepal Tree Press), which won the Guyana Prize for a first book. This was followed by a second collection, *Fabula Rasa* (Peepal Tree Press, 1992).

Faustin Charles (Trinidad and Tobago) b. 1944; story-teller, critic and novelist as well as a much admired poet. He made his reputation as a poet with the collections *The Expatriate* (1969) and *Crab Track* (1973) (both Brookside Press) but he has also written two novels, a book of stories and a children's book. His most recent publications are the collection of poems *Days and Nights in the Magic Forest* (Bogle L'Overture, 1986) and his novel *The Black Magic Man of Brixton* (Karnak House, 1985). He reads some of his poems on the disc entitled *Come From That Window Child* (see p 236).

LeRoy Clarke (Trinidad and Tobago) b. 1938; one of Trinidad's most accomplished painters. In 1980 he published a vividly illustrated collection of poems, *Douens* – described as 'Clarke's Scriptures' – from which 'Soucouyant' is taken (Karaele, 1981).

Merle Collins (Grenada) was a teacher in Grenada before moving to the UK in 1983. She now lectures in Caribbean Studies at North London Polytechnic. With Rhonda Cobham she edited *Watchers and Seekers* (Women's Press, 1987) an anthology of poetry and fiction by black women in Britain. She has also published a novel, *Angel* (Women's Press, 1987) a collection of stories, *Rain Darling* (Women's Press, 1987) and a book of poems, *Because the Dawn Breaks* (Karia Press, 1985).

Christine Craig (Jamaica) b. 1948; member of the 'Caribbean Artists Movement' in London in the 1960s and subsequently worked for the Women's Bureau in Jamaica. She has written film and TV scripts, published two children's books and a collection of poems, *Quadrille for Tigers* (Mina Press, 1984). She now lives in the USA.

Cyril Dabydeen (Guyana) b. 1945; made his name as a poet in Guyana, winning several prestigious prizes in the 1960s. He moved to Canada in 1970 and teaches at Algonquin College and the University of Ottawa. His recent work includes the poetry collections *Islands Lovelier Than a Vision* (Peepal Tree Press, 1986), and *Selected Poems* (Mosaic Press, 1990). Recent fiction includes *Dark Swirl* (Peepal Tree Press, 1989), *The Wizard Swami* (Peepal Tree Press, 1989) and *To Monkey Jungle* (Third Eye Press, 1989).

David Dabydeen (Guyana) b. 1955; has been lecturer in the Centre for Caribbean Studies at the University of Warwick and is currently Director of the Centre for Research into Asian Migration there. He has several scholarly books to his credit, including *Hogarth's Blacks* (Dangaroo Press, 1985), two books of poems, *Slave Song* (Dangaroo Press, 1984) – which won the Commonwealth Poetry Prize – and *Coolie Odyssey* (Dangaroo Press, 1990). He also published a controversial novel, *The Intended* (Secker & Warburg, 1990). He reads a selection from his own poems on the *Bluefoot Cassettes* and on the record *Come From That Window Child* (details p 236).

Fred D'Aguiar (Guyana) b. 1960; was born in London but brought up in Guyana. A dramatist and critic as well as a poet, his first book of poems, *Mama Dot* (Chatto Poetry, 1985) won wide critical acclaim and several important prizes. His second collection, *Airy Hall* (Chatto Poetry) was published in 1989. He reads a selection of his work on the *Bluefoot Cassettes* (details p 236).

Mahadai Das (Guyana) grew up in Guyana but left to study in Canada. After serious illness she returned to Guyana, where she continues to write. She has published three collections, most recently *Bones* (Peepal Tree Press, 1988).

Gloria Escoffery (Jamaica) b. 1923; painter, teacher and art critic. An original and underrated poet, over four decades her work has been scattered through many journals and anthologies. A pamphlet, *Landscape in the Making* was published in 1976 and a collection, *Loggerhead*, (Sandberry Press) in 1988.

John Figueroa (Jamaica) b. 1920; has held chairs and lectured at universities in the Caribbean, Africa, Europe and the USA. Among his many publications on education, literature, language and cricket are four collections of poetry spanning almost half a century, most recently *The Chase* (Peepal Tree Press, 1992). His *Caribbean Voices* anthologies (Evans, 1966/70) remain important resources for students of West Indian literature. He currently lives in England, where he continues to write, broadcast and lecture on a freelance basis.

Honor Ford-Smith (Jamaica) b. 1951; actress, playwright and critic as well as a fine poet. She teaches at the Jamaica School of Drama and is perhaps best known as Artistic Director of the Sistren Theatre Collective. She is editor and co-author of Sistren's *Lionheart Gal: Life Stories of Jamaican Women* (Women's Press, 1986). She hasn't yet published a collection of her own poetry but her work is included in several important anthologies.

Anson Gonzalez (Trinidad and Tobago) b. 1936; teacher, editor and broadcaster. He has been a crucial catalyst in the development of Caribbean writing through the 1970s and '80s by his editorship of *The New Voices*. His publications include *Collected Poems* (1979), *Postcards and Haiku* (1984) and *Moksha: Poems of Light and Sound* (1988), all published by New Voices.

Lorna Goodison (Jamaica) b. 1947; artist and poet. Her collections of poems – and her readings from them – have won international acclaim. Her most recent collections are *I Am Becoming My Mother* (1986) and *Heartease* (1989), both published by New Beacon Books, who have also issued a cassette of her reading from her poetry. She has also published a collection of short stories, *Baby Mother and the King of Swords* (Longman, 1990).

Jean Goulbourne (Jamaica) works in the Ministry of Education in Jamaica. She has published two collections, *Actors in the Arena* (Savacou Poets, 1977) and *Under The Sun* (New Voices, 1985).

Cecil Gray (Trinidad and Tobago) b. 1923; anthologist and lecturer in the Department of Education, University of the West Indies, Jamaica. His important anthologies for schools have helped shape the literary taste of a generation of Caribbean students. His own poems and stories are scattered through many journals and anthologies. He now lives in Canada.

A. L. Hendriks (Jamaica) 1922–1992; a much travelled poet and broadcaster who published eight collections over the years, including *To Speak Simply: Selected Poems 1961–86* (Hippopotamus Press, 1988).

Kendel Hippolyte (Saint Lucia) b. 1952; perhaps the outstanding Caribbean poet of his generation. He studied at the University of the West Indies in Jamaica and works now at the Folk Research Centre in Castries. He edited *Confluence: Nine Saint Lucian Poets* (The Source, Castries, 1988) and *So Much Poetry in We People* (Eastern Caribbean Popular Theatre Organisation, 1990) an anthology of performance poetry from across the Eastern Caribbean. He has published two collections, *Island in the Sun, Side Two* (1980) and *bearings* (1986).

Abdur Rahman Slade Hopkinson (Guyana) b. 1934; educated in Barbados and at the University of the West Indies in Jamaica, he was a teacher in Trinidad and lectured at the University of Guyana before moving to Canada in 1977. He has published three collections of poetry, including *The Madwoman of Papine* (1976).

Arnold H. Itwaru (Guyana) b. 1942; has lived in Toronto since 1969. He has published three widely-admired collections of poetry, *Shattered Songs* (Aya Press, Toronto, 1982), *Entombed Survivals* (Williams Wallace, 1987) and *body rites (beyond the darkening)* (Tsar Press, 1991) and a novel, *Shanti* (Peepal Tree Press, 1988). He is also the author of two scholarly books on the subject of power and mass communication, and a work of literary criticism, *The Invention of Canada: Literary Texts and the Immigrant Imagination* (Tsar Press, Toronto, 1990).

Amryl Johnson (Trinidad and Tobago) spent her early childhood in Trinidad but emigrated to Britain when she was eleven. In recent years she has done much teaching of creative writing but has also spent more and more time back in the Caribbean. She is best known as a poet, her collection *Long Road to Nowhere* (Virago, 1985) winning wide acclaim. She also published an autobiographical essay, *Sequins on a Ragged Hem* (Virago, 1988). In 1991 Cofa Press, Coventry issued *Blood and Wine*, a cassette of her readings from her own work, and *Tread Carefully in Paradise*, which collected her early poetry in one volume. She has just published a new collection of poems, *Gorgons* (Cofa Press, 1992).

Linton Kwesi Johnson (Jamaica) b. 1952; moved to Britain in 1963. He is a cultural activist, a member of the Race Today collective, and is committed to the performance and recording of his work. His collections include *Voices of the Living and the Dead* (Race Today, 1973), *Dread Beat and Blood* (Bogle L'Overture, 1975), *Englan is a Bitch* (Race Today, 1980) and most recently his selected poems, *Tings an Times* (Bloodaxe Books, 1991). Much of his work is available on record or cassette, most recently *Tings an Times* (Stern Records, 1991) and a selection is included on the *Bluefoot Cassettes* (details p. 236).

E. McG. 'Shake' Keane (St. Vincent) b. 1927 (as Ellsworth McGranahan Keane); internationally admired jazz musician, teacher and highly original writer. His collection, *One A Week With Water* won the Casa de las Americas prize in 1979. He has also published *The Volcano Suite* (Reliance Press, St. Vincent, 1979).

Paul Keens-Douglas (Trinidad and Tobago) b. 1942; actor and acclaimed performer of his work which he has taken all over the Caribbean and further afield. His collections include *When Moon Shine, Tim Tim* and *Tell Me Again* (all Keensdee Publications). His work is also available on several records and cassettes issued by Good Vibes Records & Music Ltd.

Anthony Kellman (Barbados) b. 1958; grew up in Barbados and graduated from the University of the West Indies. He currently teaches Creative Writing at Augusta College in Georgia, USA. He has published stories and essays but is best known as a poet. His finest work is collected in *Watercourse* (Peepal Tree Press, 1990).

Jane King (Saint Lucia) b. 1952; teaches at the Sir Arthur Lewis Community College in Castries. In recent years she has published stories and poems in several regional journals and anthologies. A selection of her poems is included in the anthology *Confluence: Nine Saint Lucian Poets* and a collection of her poetry is forthcoming.

John Robert Lee (Saint Lucia) b. 1948; drama critic, preacher, librarian, teacher and general 'man of letters' in Saint Lucia. He is at present engaged in compiling a bibliography of Saint Lucian literature. He has published several collections of his poetry, most recently *Saint Lucian* (Phelps Publications, 1988) and *Clearing Ground* (New Life Fellowship, Boston 1991).

E. A. Markham (Montserrat) b. 1939; widely-travelled and original poet. He edited the journal *Artrage* for some years and produced the anthology *Hinterland* (Bloodaxe, 1989). His own poetry is widely published and collected in several books, including his *Selected Poems 1970–82, Human Rites* (Anvil Press, 1984) and *Towards the End of a Century* (Anvil Press Poetry, 1989). He reads a selection of his poems on the *Bluefoot Cassettes* (details p 236).

Marc Matthews (Guyana) b. 1937; grew up in Guyana where he worked in broadcasting and drama. He has also been an actor and with Ken

Corsbie formed the performance duo Dem Two, which had great success right across the Caribbean. He settled in Britain in 1984 and currently works with the probation service. His first collection of poems, *Guyana My Altar*, won the Guyana Prize for a first book of poetry in 1987.

Marina Ama Omowale Maxwell (Trinidad and Tobago) b. 1934; best known perhaps as founder of the influential Yard Theatre Company in Jamaica in the 1960s, she has also been an important figure in the Caribbean Artists' Movement and the Writers' Union in Trinidad. She is an independent video producer/director/writer and a lecturer in communications. Her publications include *The Weakened Sex, About Our Own Business* and *Chopstix in Mauby*.

Ian McDonald *see the first page of this book.*

Anthony McNeill (Jamaica) b. 1941; journalist and creative writing tutor, whose poetry has been widely praised. His collections include *Reel from 'The Life Movie'* (Savacou, 1972) and *Credences at the Altar of Cloud* (Institute of Jamaica, 1979). He co-edited, with Neville Dawes, the Carifesta anthology *The Caribbean Poem*, (Institute of Jamaica, 1976). He reads a selection of his poems on the record *Poets from the West Indies* (details p 236).

Mark McWatt (Guyana) lectures in the Dept of English at the University of the West Indies, Barbados. A respected literary critic, he is one of the editors of the *Journal of West Indian Literature*. He has published one much praised collection of his poetry, *Interiors* (Dangaroo Press, 1989).

Pauline Mclville (Guyana) is an actress and writer. Her first collection of stories, *Shapeshifter* (Women's Press, 1990) won the Commonwealth Literature Prize and the Guyana Prize for a first book. She has not yet published a collection of poems but a selection of her work is included in the anthology *Rented Rooms*, (ed. D. Dabydeen, Dangaroo Press, 1988).

Ras Michael (Guyana) is a poet, storyteller, actor and teacher of drama. Also editor of the magazine *Survival*, and publisher of *Black Chant*. He has also become a memorable chronicler of urban street-people after hours in his regular column written for *Stabroek News* in Guyana.

Rooplall Monar (Guyana) b. 1945; grew up on a sugar estate in Guyana and has worked as a teacher, an estate book keeper, a journalist and a healer. He has published a novel, *Janjhat* (1989), two collections of stories, *Backdam People* (1985) and *High House and Radio* (1992) and a collection of poems, *Koker* (1987), all published by Peepal Tree Press.

Pamela Mordecai (Jamaica) b. 1942; writes, runs the family business and develops language arts textbooks. She has edited several anthologies including *Her True-True Name* (Heinemann, 1989 – with Betty Wilson).

Her first collection of poetry, *Journey Poem* (Sandberry Press) was published in 1989.

Mervyn Morris (Jamaica) b. 1937; critic, anthologist and Reader in West Indian Literature in the Department of English at the University of the West Indies, Jamaica, as well as being one of the Caribbean's major contemporary poets. He edited *The Faber Book of Contemporary Caribbean Short Stories* (Faber, 1990) and *Seven Jamaican Poets* (Bolivar Press, 1971) and co-edited the poetry anthologies *Jamaica Woman* (Heinemann, 1980) with Pamela Mordecai, and *Voiceprint* (Longman, 1989) with Gordon Rohlehr and Stewart Brown. He has published three collections of his own poetry: *The Pond* (1973) and *Shadow Boxing* (1979), both published by New Beacon Books and *On Holy Week* ('Pathways', UWI, Jamaica, 1988). He reads a selection of his early poems on the disc *Poets from the West Indies* (details p 236).

Philip Nanton (St. Vincent) b. 1947; lectures in the Institute of Local Government at Birmingham University. As well as writing poetry, he co-edited, with Nick Toczek and Yann Lovelock, the anthology of pan-Caribbean writing *Melanthika* (Little Word Machine, 1975) and was joint author, with Veronica Wanton, of *Anancy's Magic* (Longman Star Plays, 1987).

Grace Nichols (Guyana) b. 1950; novelist and children's writer as well as a poet. She has published a novel, *Whole of a Morning Sky* (Virago, 1986) but is best known for her collections of poetry: *i is a long-memoried woman* (Karnac House, 1983) won the Commonwealth Poetry Prize in 1983, *The Fat Black Woman Poems* (Virago, 1984) and *Lazy Thoughts of a Lazy Woman* (Virago, 1989). She reads a selection of her poems on the cassette *Contemporary Literature on Cassette 1* and *Come From That Window Child* (details p 236).

Sasenarine Persaud (Guyana) grew up in Guyana but at present lives and works in Canada. An outspoken critic as well as a writer, he has published two novels, *Dear Death* (1990) and *The Ghost of Bellow's Man* (1992), and a collection of poems, *Demerary Telepathy* (1988), all published by Peepal Tree Press.

Velma Pollard (Jamaica) b. 1937; lectures in Language Education at the University of the West Indies, Jamaica. She edited the schools anthologies *Over Our Way* (Longman, 1980), and *Anansesem* (Longman, Jamaica, 1985). She has also published a collection of stories, *Considering Woman* (Women's Press, 1989) and a book of poems, *Crown Point* (Peepal Tree Press) in 1988.

Victor D. Questel (Trinidad and Tobago) 1949–82; dramatist and literary critic, breaking important new ground with his poetry when he died at the tragically young age of 33. His collections include *Score*, with

Anson Gonzalez, (1972), *On Mourning Ground* (1979), and *Hard Stares* (1982), all published by The New Voices Press in Diego Martin, Trinidad.

Rajandaye Ramkissoon-Chen (Trinidad and Tobago) is a gynaecologist and obstetrician who began writing in the mid-1980s. Her poems have been published in journals and anthologies in the USA and across the Caribbean.

Andrew Salkey (Jamaica) b. 1928; the quintessential Caribbean writer, perhaps best known for his novels *Escape to an Autumn Pavement* (1960), *Come Home, Malcolm Heartland* (Hutchinson, 1976) and *The Late Emancipation of Jerry Stover* (Longman, 1982). He is also a diarist, critic and editor of important collections like his *Stories from the Caribbean* (1965) and the landmark poetry anthology, *Breaklight* (Hamish Hamilton, 1971). He has also published several volumes of poetry, including *Jamaica* (Hutchinson, 1974) *Away* (Allison & Busby, 1980) and *In the Hills Where Her Dreams Live* (Black Scholar Press, 1981). In 1992 Bogle L'Overture published *Ananey Traveller*, a collection of stories. Since 1976 Salkey has been Professor of Writing in the School of Humanities and Arts at Hampshire College, University of Amherst, USA.

Dennis Scott (Jamaica) 1939–91; playwright, actor, dancer and teacher. His poetry is collected in the prizewinning *Uncle Time* (University of Pittsburg Press, 1973), *Dreadwalk* (New Beacon Books, 1982), and *Strategies* (Sandberry Press, 1989). He reads a selection of his poems on the *Poets from the West Indies* disc (details p 236).

Olive Senior (Jamaica) b. 1941; grew up in rural Jamaica and much of her work grows out of that experience. She has been editor of *Jamaica Journal*, and published several works on aspects of Caribbean culture. Since her first collection of stories, *Summer Lightning* (Longman, 1986) won the Commonwealth Literature Prize, she has travelled widely and made her living as a writer. She published a second collection of stories, *The Arrival of the Snake Woman* (Longman, 1989) and a book of poems, *Talking of Trees* (Calabash Publications, Kingston, 1985).

A. J. Seymour (Guyana) 1914–89; one of the great men of Caribbean poetry. A critic as well as a poet, he founded and edited the literary magazine *Kyk-over-al*, which ran for more than a decade and was revived, with co-editor Ian McDonald, in the early 1980s. He edited several anthologies, particularly of Guyanese poetry, and published many collections of his own poems over forty years. Perhaps the most accessible collection of his poetry is included in the volume of essays and tributes, *AJS at 70* (ed. Ian McDonald, 1984), published to celebrate Seymour's seventieth birthday. A full *Collected Poems* is at present being edited by Ian McDonald for future publication.

Jonathan Small (Barbados) is a librarian in Barbados, and has published two collections of poetry, *the pig-sticking season* (Kellman Publications, 1986) and *Death of a Pineapple Salad* (1987), his selected poems 1976–86.

Michael Smith (Jamaica) 1954–83; perhaps the best known and most subtle of the dub poets; his performances caused a sensation wherever he appeared. He was cruelly murdered – stoned to death – by political thugs in Jamaica. He reads from his work on the discs *An Evening of International Poetry* (details below) and his own recording *Mi C-YaaN beLieVe iT* (Island Records, 1982) carries the text of his poems on its sleeve. A collection of Michael Smith's work, *It A Come*, edited and introduced by Mervyn Morris, was published by Race Today Publications in 1986.

Ralph Thompson, (Jamaica) b. 1928; a painter as well as a successful businessman and poet. His poems have appeared in journals in the USA and the UK as well as across the Caribbean in recent years, and his first collection, *The Denting of a Wave* was published by Peepal Tree Press in 1992.

Derek Walcott (Saint Lucia) b. 1930; playwright, painter and cultural critic, as well as perhaps the region's most accomplished poet. He has published three collections of plays and more than a dozen individual books of poems, most recently his *Collected Poems 1948–84* (Faber, 1986), *The Arkansas Testament* (Faber, 1988) and *Omeros* (Faber, 1990). He reads a selection from his work on the anthology records, *Poets from the West Indies* and *Poetry International* (details below).

Anthology recordings on disc and cassette

An Evening of International Poetry eds. John La Rose and Linton Kwesi Johnson, Alliance Records, 1983.

Poetry International ed. Peter Orr, Argo, 1971.

Poets from the West Indies Reading Their Own Work ed. John Figueroa, Caedmon Records, 1971.

Bluefoot Cassettes ed. James Berry, British National Sound Archive, 1990.

Contemporary Literature on Cassette, *1* (featuring the work of Grace Nichols and Sam Selvon), British National Sound Archive, 1990.

Come From That Window Child, Bogle L'Overture, 1986.